ADVERTISING

THE FORGOTTEN YEARS

Millais' famous *Bubbles*, 23 August 1912. Millais was the first Academician to have a painting bought for advertising. The buyer was Thomas J. Barratt of A. & F. Pears

ADVERTISING

THE FORGOTTEN YEARS

BY **ERIC FIELD**

LONDON
ERNEST BENN LIMITED

First published 1959 by Ernest Benn Limited
Bouverie House · Fleet Street · London · EC4

Printed in Great Britain

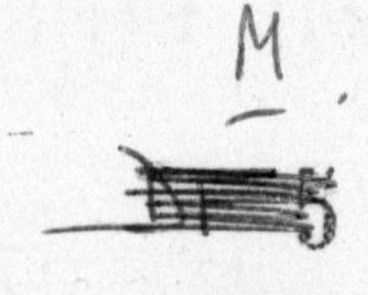

Preface

THE REASON I am trying to write this story about advertising in the first quarter of the twentieth century is that the longer I live the more annoyed do I become when I read stories by quite important people suggesting that no one knew anything about advertising till after the first World War.

I am convinced that for the benefit of future historians someone should put some of the *facts* on record in a permanent form.

Within the last year or so, for instance, I have read that the only reason J. Walter Thompson took down their plate during the first World War was because there was no Government advertising. Apart from being a gross libel on a very fine firm, it was ridiculously untrue. The Government spent hundreds of thousands of pounds on all forms of advertising during that war.

I have seen even the *Advertiser's Weekly* give a banner heading 'First ever whole pages for the Government' as a description of the Civil Defence advertising, forty-three years after the Government took its first whole pages.

In a similarly august journal I learnt, on the authority of a high executive of one of our biggest agencies, that it was only after the first World War that agents ceased to be anything but space brokers and that it was only between 1926 and 1930 that agents, whose activities till then had been limited to press advertising, began to take any interest in posters and other forms of advertising.

To make this nonsense even worse, his own firm was well established by 1895 and had designed, printed and exhibited very striking posters in the early nineteen hundreds, among them those of the famous Kodak Girl with her striped frock.

Although I have received great help from others as to details and dates, I am sorry that this has perforce to be something of an autobiography of one whose life does not contain a great deal of interest to anyone but himself.

Although I am trying to cover the first twenty-five years of the century, my own entry into the business was in 1905.

Ten years before that, *The Times* had on its books nearly 100 advertising agents, of whom at least fifty are still in business.

In 1895 most, if not all, of these were merely space brokers content to sell a paper's space and draw their commission. Many of them had sole concessions for one or more publications.

By 1905 all the best of them had become in varying degrees service agents in the modern sense of the word, though many of them retained some or all of their sole concessions.

The names of some of the survivors of 1895 include, in no particular order,

> Haddon's, Street's, Mitchell's, Keymer's, Mather and Crowther, Gordon & Gotch, Pool's (now Murray's), Sell's, T. B. Browne, Dixon's West End, Smith's, Vernon's, L.P.E., Benson's and my own little Erwoods.

In addition during the following ten years, several purely service agents had been established.

Finally, I am, so far as is possible, confining my story to the period to 1926, because there are many others who know the details of the momentous events since then much better than I do.

December 1958 E. F.

Contents

Illustrations

[*See note on use of these specimens, from the* Daily Mail, *on page 121*]

1. My Early Days

MY ENTRANCE into advertising was accidental. If the Battle of Waterloo was won on the playing fields of Eton, Eric Field's future was settled on the muddy Rugger fields of Dulwich.

At that time I was studying shorthand, précis writing and so on at Skerry's College in Croydon, the idea being that I should begin as a second-class Civil Servant and gradually work my way into becoming a first-class one and a high-up in the Foreign Office.

Fortunately for me, one Ashby Goodall came down with my father, who was then on the staff of the old *Westminster Gazette*, to watch Goodall's old school, Bedford, fight a draw with my old school, Dulwich. Draws for that match were our speciality and, I believe, still are.

Goodall asked my father what he was planning for his son and, learning of the dire fate ahead of him, said, 'For Heaven's sake don't. I'll give him a job in my business!'

So in April 1905, I joined the Spottiswoode Advertising Agency in Clun House, Surrey Street, Strand.

'Spotts' was an offshoot of the well-known printing firm of Spottiswoode & Co. About a year earlier, under the Chairmanship of John Spottiswoode, the printing company had established a special department to supply copy and artwork for its clients and, even more, for its potential clients.

Directors' disagreements led to John's resignation and he took part of the service staff and started the advertising agency at the beginning of 1905. His one co-director was Ashby Goodall. H. E. (later Sir Herbert) Morgan took the rest of the staff and set up a similar service for W. H. Smith and Sons' printing department.

By modern standards 'Spotts' was a comic opera. At the time I joined, it occupied no less than four small rooms. Its entire personnel was John Spottiswoode and Ashby Goodall as directors, Brame Hillyard, C. K. Maconochie and an unknown Australian, J. Murray Allison, as what we then called 'canvassers', a space buyer, Jack Hurle, from T. B. Browne, a book-keeper, a couple of typists and two office boys, including me. No studio, no copy department, no research or any of the other services now regarded as essential.

But that little Agency played a big part in the growth of British advertising.

Spottiswoode himself carried out no very active role in the business. All I remember of him is a long, lean figure who had the invariable habit, whenever he went out, of returning in five minutes' time for something he'd 'forgotten'. If he had come back a second time, he might have caught the mice at play, but he never did and the mice soon learned their lesson.

Ashby Goodall on the other hand played a very important part. He was incidentally a nephew of Sir George Newnes, founder of the famous publishing house. Goodall was the main inspiration of the little concern in its early stages and Advertising suffered a grave loss when, six years later, he took a toss off his Indian motor cycle and died from a broken spine. Had he lived he would have written his name large in the annals of advertising. His younger brother was the Toby Goodall who in later years made us desire White Horse Whisky even more than we should have done in any event.

But the one member of that little firm who turned out to be the most outstanding character of all that early epoch was J. Murray Allison. Jim, whose father was manager of His Majesty's Theatre in Sydney, had come over from Australia at the suggestion of Thomas Russell, who was then the Advertisement Manager of *The Times*. Unfortunately, by the time Allison arrived, Russell had ceased to occupy that chair and Jim had to fend for himself in the Old Country. Finding that, even if the streets of London were paved with gold, open-cast mining was not encouraged in the Strand, he eked out a precarious living by drawing the menus for a feeding house in the Euston Road. One day, he was fond of telling us, he did himself out of a meal by doing a menu so good that it lasted for two days.

In those times, of course, there were no restrictions on canvassing. You could call on anyone you liked, write to anyone you chose, criticise his advertising at your will and not only offer to, but press him to let you submit your suggestions for his advertising. No one had even heard of the words 'adequate fee'.

And if you wanted to get business by cutting commission, there was no one to suggest that it was wrong.

Jim Allison didn't find it necessary to cut commission, but he did everything else. My very first job for him was to cut out and paste up some proofs of type-settings on to some photographs of women in feather boas for Debenham & Freebody's. I did it so minutely that you could not detect where photograph finished and proof began, but we never got the account.

This plan of submitting new advertisements worked pretty well in those days, because the average quality and appearance of current copy was very low. There wasn't much to beat in the way of competition then and it was much easier to produce something which looked quite outstanding than it is now.

At that time, too, it was probably a good way for business to be transferred. The thought put into advertising was only beginning to go deeper than the construction of the actual advertisements. Questions of real policy seldom arose. Marketing and merchandising were equally seldom regarded as worthy of serious consideration or careful planning. If they were, it was very rare to find them linked in any way to the advertising and it was a common occurrence to find that the man responsible for the selling was hardly on speaking terms with whoever was entrusted with the advertising. Jealousy was much more common than co-operation, while it was almost unknown for the advertising agent to be given any confidential figures about sales or results.

Most advertising agents, indeed, would not have known what to do with such figures had they received them. They were content to act as space buyers, producing a list of papers, quoting the special rates they could secure and inserting in them whatever copy the agent was able to construct or the advertiser to supply.

Rates were often the overwhelming consideration. Few papers adhered rigidly to their printed scales and every agent strove to secure better terms than his competitor. At times one would be forced to charge the client less on some important paper than one actually paid, hoping to make up on the swings what one had lost on the roundabouts.

That bad principle, at least, vanished with the first World War. I do not suggest it was wrong to try to buy space at less than card rates. Far from it! Most papers asked too much for their space. But it was, and is, wrong for the agent to make an extra profit on one paper to counter-balance a loss on another, and the undue emphasis on rates of old led to an under-emphasis on all the more important factors.

Spottiswoode's had to strive to hold their own in such matters, but they were one of the early agencies which were purely service agencies and among the forerunners of the advertising agency as we know it today.

They had never heard of Market Investigation or Research but they did try to put real thought *behind* an advertising campaign. They did urge upon the advertiser the importance of close co-operation between advertising and sales departments. They worked out mailing matter and broadsheets to the retailer and saw to their production and despatch where the client had no facilities to do so himself.

They were revolutionary enough even to suggest that show

material and salesmen's aids ought to be closely related to the press advertising.

It is only in retrospect that I appreciate all these things. I was just an odd-job lad, turning a hand to anything that turned up, running errands, checking vouchers, doing up parcels and so on.

In a lot of ways the routine work was much simpler then. As a rule schedules were settled in all their details for twelve-month periods. The schedule would be prepared and orders placed for a year; the copy approved and despatched for the same period and no changes would be made till the next year's campaign came along. In those days, too, papers inserted advertisements on the day you told them to. So, even for a year ahead, orders for daily papers would be placed for specified days, which usually avoided Saturdays and always avoided Bank Holidays. On such days the papers would often carry little but large spaces at heavily cut rates. If you saw a whole page of Kutnow's in a big daily on a holiday you could be sure it was a half-price bargain. Sigismund Kutnow was a very keen bargainer!

Under such free and unrestricted conditions Allison found his real opportunity. The business he got for the little agency was quite remarkable. In the space of a few months such names as Rudge-Whitworth Cycles, Spillers' Turog Bread, Wood Milne Rubber Heels, at that time the leader in the trade, Waring & Gillow and others equally imposing appeared on our books.

As Allison was paid mainly on commission—his basic salary was, I believe, £3 a week—and as most of this business was his, the commission he earned presented quite a problem. So the Board, in other words Spottiswoode and Goodall, paid him largely in shares and made him a director. Within a few months the same problem rose again and was solved in the same way. This time he became senior to Goodall.

Incidentally, I received an unexpected windfall—two 'rises' in one week. On the Thursday evening that Allison won his second promotion I was licking stamps, when he came into the room flushed with triumph. He asked me what I was getting and, when I replied, 'Twenty shillings a week Sir', said, 'Oh, that's not enough. I'll make it twenty-two and six.' I did not think it necessary to mention that I had had a five shilling rise only on the Monday!

One factor in his success was the quality of our art work. We had no studio of our own but Goodall and Allison had made friends with two young Canadians, Bill Wallace and Archie Martin.

They had come over to England on a holiday and had been surprised to find that the modern conception of a commercial studio was practically unknown here.

The result was that they seized the opportunity and established what they named the Carlton Studio. Spottiswoode's became their first agency client and for a time had the exclusive call on their services for agency work.

The combination worked well. So often were we in communication that I still remember their telephone number—Central 12888! They were charming lads and deservedly successful.

Exclusive arrangements, however, are seldom entirely satisfactory and after a while a new studio, called the Grafton Studio, sprang into being, doing exactly the same type of work and under the same ownership.

We knew all about it and nobody cared.

It was not long before Spottiswoode's outgrew the accommodation available at Clun House and we moved to Oswaldestre House, Norfolk Street.

There we enrolled two new recruits. One was Fred Akerman, who later on became Advertisement Manager of *The Times Weekly Edition*. Fred was in my opinion the nicest of the three Akerman brothers. He was an expert on print and became more or less the office manager. His salary was no less than £500 a year. I know this because somehow the letter appointing him slipped into the ordinary filing system and it gave me my first realisation that there was real money in this advertising business.

The other was W. C. Pelot. One day Goodall told me with great pride that the firm had engaged the greatest copy writer in London. Bill Pelot may not have been that but he certainly was a good one.

He came to us from the Paul E. Derrick Co. who were in the same building. Pelot, like Paul Derrick, was an American and even in those days American advertising men meant something in England.

The Derrick agency, largely aided by, I think it was, the Quaker Oats account, was quite important. From it sprang the Powell Rees Agency which later on closed down. Derrick's itself at one time went under the wing of Crawford's but after leaving that shelter ran into trouble and packed up. It was at Oswaldestre House, too, that I first met Thornton Bridgwater who later achieved fame on the *Draper's Record.*

After a year or two in Oswaldestre House, Spottiswoode's amalgamated with Dixon & Hunting Ltd. of 180 Fleet Street.

The moving gave me quite a thrill. I was entrusted with the job of supervising the mechanics of the move. I spent my first night in a hotel, the Howard in Norfolk Street.

At eight in the morning the moving started. I still remember seeing men on horseback coming through the mist in Fleet Street on their way to the Park. The nearest I have been to that since then was the 'pink' I was to see years later from 30 Fleet Street in the back windows of Hoare's Bank. It was said to be a tradition that the head of that old family business should live on the premises and be a keen follower of the hounds.

The amalgamation, known as Spottiswoode, Dixon & Hunting, brought several new characters into my acquaintance. John Spottiswoode passed out of the picture. In his place came Proctor Humphris, later to be the Major Proctor Humphris of Industrial Publicity, which led me in an unguarded moment after the first World War to have a special edition of my business visiting card with the title

Lieut.-Colonel. I think I used it once just for the purpose of calling on my one-time boss!

Dixon was dead or retired. Hunting was breeding pheasants in Norfolk. Otherwise the directorate was as before but new faces came into the office.

Jimmy Walton Harvey was one of them. If my memory is correct he was then in charge of motoring advertisements for the *Morning Post*, which at that time still refused illustrated advertisements. Marcus Heber Smith of the Norfolk Studio was another. Various friends of Jim Allison's Australian days would crop up every now and then. Ernest Mozar is the one I remember most, perhaps because later on we worked together on *The Times*.

Mozar had been an actor and among his fund of anecdotes was that of the night in Newcastle when, after playing the lead in a costume comedy called *Monsieur Beaucaire*, he was met at the stage door by a Northumbrian miner's remark, 'Call yourself a b——y comedian! My b——y foot, you ain't.'

'Mo', having forsaken the stage for advertising, professed to feeling flattered at being mistaken for his better known contemporary, George Mozart.

We all wondered if he did. In those days there was a wide gap between a juvenile lead in a touring 'legitimate' and even a 'top-liner' on the Halls.

About this time I got to know Philip Benson, who played for an old Alleynian rugger team of which I happened to be captain. One day he asked me if I would like a job with S. H. Benson Ltd. Seeing a chance to widen my experience I accepted and a few weeks later I joined the old firm as a junior copy writer at, I think, £2 a week, in the fire-trap of a wooden building they then occupied in Tudor Street; very different from the premises to which they shortly moved in one of the first buildings to be completed in Kingsway.

When I joined the firm in 1908, Benson's were full service agents in the modern meaning of the word. They had long since ceased to be space brokers, if they ever had served that function, and depended for their success on the service they provided for the advertiser. Even at that time they had their own poster inspection organisation.

The nearest they got to space broking was the use of carriers' vans. At this period these vans wandered all round the countryside selling hardware, groceries and all sorts of things. In a very much smaller degree they exist today.

Somehow or other Benson had fixed up a deal with a funny little Baptist parson, named Popham, who had built up a connection for arranging posters on such vans, to carry on the business for him. Popham, incidentally, had two charming sons, one of whom achieved fame with the *Nottingham Guardian* and the other with Smith's of 100 Fleet Street.

S. H. Benson, the founder of the firm, had originally been an officer in the Navy. Retiring from the sea, he became Advertising Manager of Bovril Ltd. and eventually, with the firm's assistance, set up as an advertising agent. For a long time the agency revolved around the Bovril account and its growth in other directions was slow.

But it was a good training ground for a young copy writer. I learned a lot from another Australian called Burriss Gahan, who later on did a very good job of work as Advertising Manager of Kodak. At Benson's, too, I worked under William H. Beable.

After a time Benson, who seemed to like me, made me his private secretary. As that I picked up a fair amount of knowledge of the conduct of an agency on a higher level, but I had reason to be glad that I did not know shorthand. Otherwise I might have drifted into being a slightly superior typist.

In 1909 Benson started the publication of an English edition of that well-known U.S. advertising journal, *Printers' Ink*, and he engaged Thomas Russell, who, having left *The Times*, had set up as Britain's first Advertising Consultant, as Editor. One day Benson gave me some notes on billposting in Wales and asked me to turn them into an article for him.

I did not realise it at the time, but Russell had asked for an assistant and this was a test to see whether I would do for the job.

Apparently I passed the test, because a week or two later I was sent to work with Russell as Assistant Editor of *Printers' Ink*. In that job I learnt a lot more than just how to run a small trade paper. Russell had been Advertising Manager of Dr. Williams' Pink Pills and knew a lot about patent medicines. In spare time I used to help him and he repaid me by passing on his knowledge. Few people could have had such an opportunity and I shall never cease to be grateful to him.

Our only direct competition in those days was a monthly called *Advertising* issued by Smith's Advertising Agency and the monthly *Advertising World* which, with a paper called *Boxing*, eventually became one of the stepping stones to success of the Berry brothers, later to be known and respected as Lord Camrose and Lord Kemsley. We had also to consider the weekly *Newspaper World* but this covered every phase of the business and advertising was only an incidental to it.

After about a year a separate company was formed for the little paper, because the newspapers had agreed that they would not be 'blackmailed' into advertising in the publications issued by some of the agents.

This hurt *Printers' Ink* pretty badly and Benson thought that an independent company with the shares held by several agents and an advertiser or two would escape the ban, as indeed in practice it did.

The company was called Printers' Ink Ltd. Its chairman was Dr. Pilley of Mellin's Food, who personally owned Mellin's Pharmacy in Piccadilly Circus. Its Managing Director and Managing Editor for the first year or so was Jesse D. Hampton who had been controller of the American *Printers' Ink*.

In June 1910 Hampton retired and returned to America.

Pilley was deputed to drop in now and then to see that the office was running all right. He was to sign the book and draw the regular director's fee of one guinea. So seriously did he take this duty that on his daily journey from Peckham to Piccadilly he dropped in every day until in ten weeks he had recouped his total investment of £50. After that we did not see him half so often.

I became Editor. As such at the mature age of twenty-two, I used to churn out about 5,000 words a week of most learned-sounding stuff on all sorts of advertising problems. I used many *noms de plume* and fortunately our readers never knew quite what a babe and suckling emitted so much wisdom.

Its main advantage to me was that the job brought me in touch with a great many people in all branches of 'The Street'. No advertising man can know too many people. You can never tell when some chance contact may not lead, perhaps quite indirectly, to business.

Having to run the paper on a shoe-string, we had to keep expenses down to a minimum. My own salary first of all was £3 per week and was increased to £4 when I became full Editor, which job I doubled with that of Secretary of the Company. It is an interesting side-light on changed conditions, that in those days one could on such a wage afford the full evening-dress in which to attend the dinners and other functions which were part of my job. The dining and speaking habit had already invaded the business. Two clubs at least were noteworthy, the Sphinx and the Thirty. I made it my business to attend all their functions, to which the Press were invited, for two reasons.

Firstly, we could not afford to send anyone else. Secondly, it gave me a chance to get to know people who might be useful to the little paper—and to me.

The Aldwych was still only an idea of Wareham Smith's. Wareham was the Advertisement Director of the *Daily Mail* group and one day he sent *Printers' Ink* a letter suggesting that a club should be set up with permanent premises. I published it with a 'leader' in support. Years later at a House Dinner in my honour I presented the Club with a framed cutting of Wareham's letter. It is still, I believe, on the walls of the Club.

During this period S. H. Benson held a sort of watching brief over the editorial policy of the little paper and after a time his interference began to make progress impossible. So the Advertisement Manager and I commenced to keep our eyes open for other opportunities. I might mention that the Advertisement Manager got the same salary as I did and that our advertising rate was £3 per page.

The Advertisement Manager, the Major William Neville Campbell I had worked with at Bensons and brought to *Printers' Ink*, and whom I years later knew as the Brigadier-General of Illustrated Newspapers, found his opportunity with the *Sphere*. Incidentally, he just missed the *Punch* job because Roy Somerville, who made such a great success on *Punch*, had had West End experience on the *Delineator*.

Mine came when one day Hedley Le Bas sent in a 'small' asking for an Advertising Manager for the Caxton Publishing Co., at that time the largest instalment publisher and the biggest mail order advertiser in the country. I wrote to him, saw him and the job was filled before the advertisement even appeared.

So Campbell and I said good-bye to the little paper almost simultaneously.

With the Caxton I had a three months' trial at £5 per week. My job was to plan the expenditure of about £20,000 a year, practically all in the six winter months, write all the copy and buy all the space. As 'publishers' we received the usual publishers' discount from nearly all the papers but, to make quite sure of it, we also ran the Caxton Advertising Agency and our order forms all carried that heading.

This was quite a job. £20,000 was a lot of money in those days and every advertisement had to pay for itself. Our biggest selling books were the *Business Encyclopaedia* and *Chambers's Illustrated Encyclopaedia*, but we had good bread-and-butter standbys, such as the *Modern Physician*, the *Musical Educator* and sets of the classics, including a so-called 'unexpurgated' edition of Balzac. Our prices ranged from thirty shillings up to £20, all payable by instalments of two and sixpence upwards.

Our principle was to offer a free booklet in the advertisements. We would follow this up with two weekly shots, the last offering the volume on approval. If my department had not received an order in three weeks, the enquiry was handed over to the canvassing department. This comprised a country-wide organisation of several score part-time canvassers on a commission basis.

We kept the most intricate accounts. Every insertion was debited with the cost of the advertisement, the printing cost of the booklet, etc., the postage and even the labour, while if an order was eventually secured by a canvasser his commission was added to the cost.

It seems complicated but it worked and in the end led Le Bas to a knighthood, about which more anon.

For me the job at the Caxton had some very useful side issues.

Except for Horatio Bottomley's *John Bull*, whose ever-varying circulation enabled us to use its columns every week of the year, there was little for me to do in the summer, and Le Bas encouraged me to take any non-competitive free-lance jobs, the firm and I sharing any fees. One year I was Assistant P.R.O. (at that time frankly and unashamedly Press Agent) for Imre Kiralfy's White City Exhibition. I also worked for two of the purely service agents. One was Charlie (later Sir Charles) Higham in his then infant but already growing agency and the other Percy Burton, who with Leslie Harwood was running the P. C. Burton & Co., which later on became the St. James's Advertising and Publishing Co., which in its turn was absorbed by the London Press Exchange, though its City office still carries on under St. James's name. One year I was advertising consultant to Whiteways, the cider people. They still survive that experience. For several years I edited the confidential circular of the Advertisers' Protection Society, the progenitor of the present I.S.B.A. I also received a retainer from Jack Akerman as a standby in case the then Editor of the *Advertising World* was unable to turn up to put the magazine to bed. Fortunately, that occasion never arose.

I should mention that Le Bas was a most remarkable man. The Jersey-born son of the Captain of one of the old 'Tea Clippers' he had enlisted as a trooper in the XVth (King's Own) Hussars. Leaving the Army as a Rough Riding Corporal, with a capital of £50, he set up in business as a 'dealer', getting orders for T. C. and E. C. Jack's technical books on the instalment plan.

So successful was he that he persuaded Jack's to help him form the Caxton Publishing Company Ltd.

Under Le Bas' energy and drive, the Company's progress was remarkable.

He was the first publisher to take the whole front page of the *Daily Mail*—in my day we took it once a month during the Season—and indeed the first publisher to use advertising in its modern sense.

It was entirely due to Le Bas' success with the Caxton that the Amalgamated Press started the Educational Book Co. and Cassell's the Waverley Book Co.

The Hedley Le Bas, who now runs the great concern in Hanover Square so successfully, is my Hedley's grandson.

2. The First Real Government Advertising

THE CAXTON also gave me the first and possibly only opportunity I have ever had to play an important part in a vital development of advertising in Britain and, indeed, in the world.

That is the use of real advertising by a National Government.

Until 1914 the British Government, like every other Government, had confined its advertising to Classified advertisements under their appropriate headings. Whether they were inviting tenders for various supplies or services or appealing for recruits for the Army or the Navy, the format and phraseology were the same.

The only exceptions were the occasional use of 'fly posting', and the stilted wording of a financial issue.

The Classified advertising was charged by the papers at 'Government Rates', which were usually higher even than the rates charged for financial advertising.

This advertising was put out for tender by the Stationery Office and at this time the contract was held by R. F. White & Son on the magnificent remuneration of 2½ per cent., the balance of the commission being returned to the Government. White's had been established in 1800 and are, I believe, the oldest established agents in the world. I know it was not till forty years later that America had its first advertising agent.

In 1913, White's noteheading still carried a charming testimonial from that famous author, Charles Lamb.

Le Bas had by now moved into high political circles with the powerful backing of Sir George Riddell of the *News of the World*, who was also a Director of the Caxton. They used to play golf at Walton Heath every Wednesday morning.

This was and is quite a good idea, which I hope to follow one day. Your secretary can tell the client who rings up in the morning, 'Oh! Mr. Jones has gone out but he will phone you this afternoon.' If, on the other hand, the client rings up about lunchtime, he may suspect that the boss who 'may not be back', has gone off for the day.

On this particular Wednesday in October 1913 something happened which marked an epoch in the history of advertising.

Le Bas and Riddell were playing with Colonel Seeley, the then Secretary of State for War. In conversation at the nineteenth hole Seeley said to Le Bas, 'You're a business man. If you were in my position and could not get enough recruits for the Army, what would you do?'

Le Bas replied, 'Advertise for them!'

I know nothing of the subsequent conversation, but you can imagine my excitement the next morning, when Le Bas told me that the Caxton Advertising Agency had been given the job of advertising for recruits, that we were authorised to spend £6,000 and to create real advertising instead of the stilted classifieds which the Government had used for a hundred years or more.

We talked the problem over. We knew that the recruiting season was very much the same as our bookselling season, because it was much easier to get a man out of work to enlist in the Army when it was too cold to hang around street corners, than in warmer months.

So we had little time to spare.

And we decided that we needed factual, down to life appeals like those we used to sell our books.

With these two basic points agreed, the little agency—and it was very little, consisting of Le Bas, a typist and me—got to work rapidly. We knew that, if we could get the papers to accept the advertising at trade rates instead of Government rates, we could afford large spaces. Between us we overcame that hurdle. So we planned for whole pages in the popular dailies, including the whole front page of the *Daily Mail* at, I believe, £350 and quad columns in the Sundays.

The schedule submitted to and approved by the War Office for January and February came to £4,000 out of our 'vote' of £6,000.

Meanwhile I wrote an advertisement headed 'What the Army offers' packed with copy and, in true Caxton tradition, finishing with a coupon offering a booklet with the same title.

We recommended a print order of 50,000, thinking that quantity would be ample for all our requirements.

By the end of the first week the War Office had run out of booklets and had to order a reprint.

This unexpected result put a severe strain on the Recruiting Staff because each enquiry was to be followed by a call from a Recruiting Sergeant. However, they managed to cope, including one enquiry from a man signing himself Evelyn Wood, who turned out to be the famous Field-Marshal of that name. What the Sergeant who called on 'Mr.' Evelyn Wood felt, history does not tell.

In the end the advertising secured an increase of 4,000 over the normal recruiting figures for the two months.

The War Office regarded this as so satisfactory that it was decided to spend £20,000 during the autumn and winter.

For this first campaign R. F. White's received their 2½ per cent., but neither Le Bas nor the Caxton received any payment.

As Seeley stated in reply to a question in the House asking why Le Bas did the work, if neither 'he nor his concern received anything at all': 'They did it from patriotic motives.'

The questioner sat down.

The first two months' campaign having been so successful we did not need to carry on for another month or two. So we at the Caxton settled down to make our plans for a winter campaign. This was to be a real campaign. Twenty thousand pounds over four months went quite a long way in those days and would allow us big spaces in a fairly wide list of papers.

And this time we were to be paid for the work.

This last fact was of considerable interest to me because by now I was to get 20 per cent. of the gross profit of the Caxton Advertising Agency, ignoring of course the Company's own work.

However, that beautiful campaign was never to come off.

Towards the end of July 1914, I, in the absence of Le Bas at Walton Heath, received a surprise call from Colonel Strachey, the A.A.G. (Recruiting). He swore me to secrecy, told me that war was imminent and that the moment it broke out we should have to start advertising at once, using as a temporary measure the £2,000 remaining out of the first vote.

That night I worked out a draft schedule and wrote an advertisement headed 'Your King and Country need you' with the inevitable Coat of Arms at the top.

Next morning Le Bas took the advertisement and the schedule to the War Office, got them approved and was told that we must remain within constant reach of the phone.

Meanwhile we were to make no move whatever, not even to get the advertisements set up, let alone book any space.

This state of suspense lasted four days. During that time Le Bas, knowing that our poor little £2,000 would only allow something like 8-inch Doubles, conceived the idea of asking publishers to insert the advertisement in the centre of their main news page.

Then, on Bank Holiday night, like thousands of others, I cheered excitedly outside Buckingham Palace. Unlike them I dashed back to the office.

The next morning Le Bas went to see Northcliffe. Northcliffe instantly agreed to Le Bas' request for *The Times*, the *Mail* and all his papers. With this example, the other publishers, some rather reluctantly, fell into line. Probably because of my youth the Editor of the *Telegraph* did not believe me when I told him of Northcliffe's promise and did not give us this unique position till next day he actually saw it in *The Times*.

One daily, now dead, would not insert our 8-inch D/C because it was carrying a whole page of the 'Stop the War' campaign.

All, however, readily followed the precedent we had set up the previous January of accepting displayed Army advertising at Trade instead of Government rates, the Agency itself returning all commission and working on a nominal payment of £10 per week.

Our first difficulty was that Kitchener, who had been recalled to the War Office while actually on the way to Egypt, was so pleased with the first advertisement that he would not allow us to vary the heading except to change it to 'Lord Kitchener needs YOU', which we did not feel was exactly an improvement, and insisted on finishing every advertisement with 'God save the King'.

When Le Bas eventually overcame this obstacle, he got together a voluntary committee consisting of J. C. Akerman, Wareham Smith, H. Simonis, Thomas Russell and Charles F. Higham, with little me, who had meanwhile been rejected for the Army on medical grounds, as secretary.

Then we really got going. Pure patriotism as a recruiting appeal soon lost its initial force. We ran the gamut of all the emotions that make men risk their lives and all the factors that deter them from doing so. '5 Questions to Employers' who were keeping gardeners who 'could be digging trenches' or chauffeurs who could be 'driving an armoured car' was a typical example. So was an advertisement to parents asking, 'What will you reply when your daughter grows up and says, "Daddy, what did you do in the Great War?" ' Those are just two which spring to my mind. No Press advertisements were illustrated. Ninety per cent. of them were about 11-inch D/C.

What made the job so exciting was that surprisingly often we could tell by recruiting figures which advertisements succeeded and which ones failed.

Once we ran quite a small campaign in Ireland with copy specially directed to Irishmen. Inside a fortnight it trebled recruiting figures in Dublin; in a month it had doubled the rate all over Ireland.

Ever since then I have believed that if advertising can make men risk their lives, there is nothing it cannot do, if properly conceived.

The best advertisements we ever wrote were a series of whole pages to launch the 'Derby Scheme'. They were never used. To this day I am convinced that had they appeared, we might never have needed conscription. Whether that would have been a good thing or not, I am far from sure.

I should make it clear that we had nothing to do with the poster campaign. This was in the hands of the Parliamentary Recruiting Committee. Indeed the only poster we got out was one for munition workers at Easter 1915. We were given the job because it was much too urgent to be left to the Committee. In twenty-four hours I took a rough down to the War Office. For the first and only time I was taken in to see Kitchener. Our rough showed a man at a lathe with a background of distant ruins. Kitchener did not like it because one of the ruins looked like a church tower. 'The British Army', he insisted, 'does not shell churches.' Anyway the poster was printed and up inside a week.

These arrangements continued right up to the introduction of conscription, which inevitably put an end to voluntary enlistment, the only exception being for technical corps.

In 1915 Reginald McKenna, the Chancellor of the Exchequer, called in Le Bas to help with the second War Loan, which had opened very unsuccessfully. Le Bas employed Thomas Russell and Charles F. Higham to write the advertisements. In three days the first of ten consecutive whole pages appeared. They were accepted at Trade rates and the saving to the Government in the ten days was over

£40,000. The Loan proved to be an outstanding success and the same arrangements persisted till the end of the war.

With some modifications they also applied to the introduction of Exchequer Bonds and War Savings Certificates, for the latter of which I designed the first book with the chart showing how each fifteen shillings and sixpence grew year by year.

On the financial advertising, by the way, we were allowed to retain 5 per cent. of the commission.

Meanwhile, of course, other Ministries had commenced to use advertising. Other agencies, other advertising men, had devoted their services to helping the National effort. Many of them are still doing so with signal success.

But it was for his work that Le Bas became the first man to receive a knighthood for purely advertising efforts.

Meanwhile, also, I had managed to wangle my way into the Army. That is a different story. Suffice it to say that I joined the Army as a private in the Royal Fusiliers and left it as a very highly paid Lieut.-Colonel, more highly paid in fact than I was as a Brigadier at G.H.Q., France, in the second World War.

3. 1918 to 1923

DURING THE first World War, when for a time I had the pleasure of serving under Percy Burton on the staff of 4th Army H.Q., I came to the conclusion that my future did not lie with the Caxton and I resolved never to take a job, if I could possibly avoid it, unless it fulfilled one of two requirements.

The first and most desirable was to allow me to have a personal stake in the business: the second was to give me a share in the fruits of my own work.

The latter was covered when Jack Akerman offered me the Advertisement Managership of a new publication he was going to start called *Nash's Weekly*.

As it happened, my demobilisation was held up and I could not get home in time to take up the position.

This may not have been so unlucky as I thought at the time. *Nash's Weekly* was just one more attempt to establish a *Saturday Evening Post* in Britain and like other previous attempts it had a short life and not a very gay one.

The delay in my 'demob' curiously enough was due to my presumed newspaper experience. The 4th Army, instead of going to Cologne, was halted in and around Namur, Charleroi and Liège. Rumour had it that the reason was because the authorities did not fancy letting our Australian Corps loose among the frauleins in Cologne.

The result was that there was no work for the troops and troops without something to do, which at least appears to be important, and nothing to interest them are bound to get slack and even undisciplined.

Our situation was not improved by the fact that the only English reading they could get was a week-old *Paris Daily Mail.*

To remedy this trouble, the D.A. and Q.M.G. (Major-General Holman) ordered me to go over to London and organise the supply of English dailies from London. In just over a week about 5,000 London dailies were being distributed all over our area the day after publication in London. And I enjoyed the, I believe, unique title of 'Army Newspaper Officer'.

This and other not very military jobs kept me in Belgium till September 1919, when I secured four days' special leave and the promise of demobilisation on my return. Four days' special leave from Namur meant two days in London.

On reaching London I found Le Bas had been trying to get in touch with me.

I rang him up and he told me *The Times* was looking for an Advertisement Manager. I phoned Howard Corbett, then General Manager, in the morning and saw him in the afternoon. I saw him again the next morning and was taken to see Lord Northcliffe. After perhaps half an hour, 'The Chief' said to Corbett, 'I like the boy. Go away and hire him!'

Back in Corbett's room, Corbett asked whether I would accept the terms my predecessor—Jack Akerman—had had. They were £1,200 a year salary, £250 expenses and 2 per cent. of the nett increase in advertising revenue on a yearly agreement. The salary and expenses were, of course, ridiculous for the responsibility of one great daily and five or six weekly papers.

On the other hand, coming from a tin-pot little town in Belgium, I knew that owing to the ban on new issues there was not a printer in London who could set up another prospectus and that any day the ban would be lifted. In which case *The Times* revenue was bound to boom.

Taking it for granted that Printing House Square realised this and knew what the 2 per cent. would mean, I said 'Yes' and went back to Belgium to get myself 'demobbed'.

There I found myself held up for a month as a vital witness in a court martial.

When I eventually did get out of uniform, the boom had started and I found myself responsible for forty-page issues of *The Times*.

My briefing was that top priority must be given to 'smalls' which were under the charge of Alfred Pemberton. Next on the list was Financial advertising under an equally able chap called Harron. Ordinary advertising came last.

That year the advertising revenue increased from £600,000 to over a million.

When I joined *The Times* I found internal staff relations and external relations far from satisfactory. Internally the advertising department at least was a hotbed of jealousy and intrigue. Had business not been so good I should have had to be ruthless and dismissed old hands who had outlived their usefulness.

One of the staff was a salesman of a type for which I have never had any use. He could sell the hind leg of the proverbial mule but he never dared go near that mule again and I did not want orders for *The Times* or its supplements from advertisers who were doomed to be dissatisfied. Incidentally, he had thought he was going to get my job, which did not help matters.

Externally, the paper was most unpopular with advertisers and particularly with advertising agents.

Fortunately, I did not have to worry about revenue and I concentrated my energies upon correcting the faults which had led to such a position.

I think that when I left the 'Old Thunderer', advertisers and agents had an entirely different feeling about the paper from the one they had before I took over.

Very soon, I realised that Howard Corbett had not appreciated what was going to happen and as the cost of newsprint and labour had increased heavily, he, being paid on nett profits, did not share my good fortune.

Not unnaturally he got jealous.

So, when the Chief came back from his last fatal journey round the world, I tried to see him to suggest a new arrangement on a longer term.

Corbett got there first and one day the telephone girl told me I was wanted by His Lordship.

In the sanctum sanctorum the conversation ran something like this: 'Field, they tell me you are unpopular. That will never do. The only reason I can go journeying round the world and leave my great businesses to run themselves is because they are all such happy families.'

'Happy Families!'

In any event the charge of being unpopular is impossible to refute. I could have justified it had I been ruthless and cleared out all dead wood in the shape of inefficient employees, but as business was so good I had erred in the other direction and unless you are told with whom you are unpopular, you are helpless.

The next thing that happened was that Lints Smith, the Associate Manager, went to Hurlingham one day with the Chief and Alfred Pemberton. There they ran into Lyle, the Sports Editor, only to hear Alfred introduced to Lyle as 'The new Advertisement Manager of *The Times*'.

L. S. duly reported this to me and the upshot was that I surrendered my remaining month or so for a couple of thousand pounds and was able to sleep peacefully at nights, without anticipating dawn phone calls from His Lordship because the *Financial Times* had carried something *The Times* had missed.

So there I was. Somewhat better off but still searching for my ideal job.

Percy Burton bobbed up again.

P. C. Burton & Co. had by this time become the St. James's Advertising and Publishing Co., a company organised by Whitcombe, who controlled among other concerns the then British Motor Corporation. Its Chairman was J. Inglis Kerr with Burton as Vice Chairman and Leslie Harwood a Director, with McLachie from A. J. Wilson as Managing

Director. Its space buyer was Freddy Gooding and his assistant the now Joe Barnett of Royds.

Among its financial clients was a firm of stockbrokers who wanted to emulate a very successful outside Broker, called Wheeler, of Leicester. Realising that they could easily get into trouble with the Stock Exchange authorities, they put it through an associated firm called the Anglo-Scottish Investment Trust, also clients of St. James's.

Burton advised them it was a two-man job, one with a knowledge of advertising, the other with experience of the City.

The result was the formation of a company called Inglis, Field & Co. Ltd.

Inglis was from St. James's. I was the Field. The little company started in most extravagant premises which had already been taken in Grosvenor Gardens. Unfortunately it started just at the beginning of the 1920 slump.

Despite that or, perhaps, because of it we managed to get business from the City and built up quite a list of clients who bought shares through us.

Then came a blow.

Our parent house, the Anglo-Scottish, had among its companies a tin mine in Wales called Aberlyn Ltd. which they told us was going to declare a big dividend and they were going to work the market. At that time the market was so slack that any real buying of shares in a company of this type would have sent the price rocketing. So we advised our clients to buy. And most of them did. Our feelings when we found that every transfer came from our parents can be imagined.

Inglis and I could not help remembering the old adage, 'Never trust nobody. Not even your own Fader.'

We decided we had learnt enough about the 'bucket-shop' business. We repaid our clients and quit the company with St. James's complete approval.

Burton and Harwood then wanted me to join St. James's but I felt they already had too many directors and I could not see with them the opportunity for which I was looking.

So we arranged that I should join them at half the salary they offered on the understanding that I could leave at short notice if I did find such an opportunity.

With them I had a mixed job. I ran what agencies then called the Copy Dept. which included the Studio. I sat in at conferences and even did some space selling. The 'space' was an ingenious moving device in trams, geared to the wheels, so that, as the tram approached an important stopping place, it showed passengers just where they were. The intervening spaces were occupied by advertisements.

I forget what we called it but, though beautiful in theory and easy for the space seller, it had troubles in practice and had a short life. Just one more idea too clever to be practicable!

On the copy side where I worked closely with John C. Kirkwood, I well remember the 'flap' when St. James's were officially informed that Dunlop were after all the years going to move from A. J. Wilson's.

There being then no ban on submitting schemes, we all worked like niggers only to learn later on that the account was going to C. F. Higham, which, had we had any sense, we should have known was a foregone conclusion.

I also remember the work the agency put in on the 'Paint more—Save more' campaign, particularly one night when I went down to Slough to be the principal speaker at a fund-raising meeting, only to find that we had walked into a building strike and that the audience was outnumbered by the platform. The meeting was not a success.

Meanwhile, I was, as mentioned, allowed to let it be known that I was open to an offer.

Various offers cropped up, including the Advertisement Directorship of what is now one of our greatest Nationals. As the terms offered meant that I should take a subordinate job under an old friend of mine for a few months and then seem to do him out of his job, I refused, unless they would pay off the then holder of the post without waiting for his agreement to run out. I still refused when the proprietor himself repeated the offer.

So I did not get the job and I have no regrets, even though the chap who got it has made a great deal of money out of it.

Eventually, the job I was looking for turned up. At the Aldwych Club I had got to know Vernon Reveley, head of W. L. Erwood Ltd. He offered me a seat on the Board and proposed to reconstruct the company so that I could acquire a substantial holding in the firm.

And that is how Erwoods Ltd. came into being in 1923, twenty-eight years after its first foundation, and how Eric Field found his resting place there.

4. How the Clubs Grew Up

EXACTLY WHEN such modern necessities as advertising clubs started in Britain I have been unable to discover.

The first advertising club ever formed in the world was the Agate Club of Chicago founded in 1894, but this was confined, like our own Fleet Street Club, to representatives of newspapers and magazines. The first to bring space sellers and space buyers together over a common board was the Sphinx Club of New York, established in 1896 and so antedating by ten years the Advertising Club of New York and the famous Poor Richard Club of Philadelphia, of which I am proud to be the senior living Honorary Member. When I was accorded that honour my companions were John Wanamaker, the famous creator of Department Stores, and our own inimitable Harry Lauder.

We formed a curious trio!

The name 'Poor Richard' was the pen name of the famous Benjamin Franklin.

Both the Poor Richard and the Advertising Club of New York are, of course, still flourishing.

The Sphinx

I am not sure just when the British Sphinx was started but it was certainly in existence in 1904, when Philip Smith of 'The Agency in a Hundred' read a paper entitled 'What is an Advertising Agent?' In it he quoted the requirements 'lately adopted by the American Newspaper Publishers' Association'. They were:

1. He shall maintain an office for the particular purpose of conducting a general advertising agency business, properly equipped.
2. He shall be financially responsible.
3. He shall have sufficient experience in the advertising business to warrant the belief that he may be successful in the conducting of a general advertising agency business.

The British Sphinx used to hold its dinners at the old Hotel Cecil on the site of the present Shell-Mex House. Its dinners were largely attended and full evening-dress affairs. When I first knew the Sphinx, its moving spirit was Ralston Balch of Scott and Bowne and its favourite humorous speaker one Mostyn Piggott.

The Thirty

The subjects discussed, however, were seldom as closely concerned with advertising as that addressed by Philip Smith and in 1905 a little group, who used to lunch together at the old Gaiety Restaurant, thought it would be a good idea to form a dining club which would treat advertising seriously.

In searching for a name, someone said, 'Well, there will never be more than thirty people in the business who don't eat peas with a knife; so let's call it the Thirty Club.'

He was a bad prophet about future table manners but that was the origin of the Club's name and the reason for its original restriction to thirty members.

The archives of the Club were lost in the 'Blitz' but I find that in writing in the *Advertiser's Weekly* in May 1923, I mentioned that the first President was John Hart and its first members included Percy Burton, Joseph Thorp, Ashby Goodall, John McBain, Oswald Green, Charles Bridges, Philip Gee and J. Murray Allison.

The motto of the Club was 'For the Betterment of Advertising' and the qualification for membership was to have done or be likely to do something to that end. Election was by ballot and two 'black balls' were one too many. In the early years more would-be members were rejected than were elected. In one year no less than nine out of ten candidates failed. (I have often wondered how I sneaked in in 1910.) One other rule was rigidly adhered to. Any member failing to attend six out of the ten monthly dinners was automatically expelled.

Election to office was also a matter of ballot and much sought after. I was for a time Hon. Secretary before the first World War and I was very proud to be elected President in 1924 after defeating Wareham Smith by one vote. As I was at the moment in the middle of the Atlantic, no one could accuse me of having cast that critical vote myself. Incidentally, I was the last President to be elected by ballot. Somebody thought such a practice was undignified.

Possibly because of the virility inspired by such a constitution, the Club played a part in the development of advertising entirely out of proportion to its size.

As far back as 1914 the Club was responsible for the formation of the British Association of Advertising under the Presidency of L. H. Hartland Swann (at that time a Managing Director of Lever Brothers). Many members of the Club visited important provincial cities to set up local advertising clubs, with the ultimate aim of holding an annual advertising convention and hoping periodically to receive the American Advertising Clubs as guests. Quite a few of the clubs existing today owe their origin to those visits. I myself can claim to have baptised the Publicity Club of Oxford.

Unfortunately, this and other activities had to be suspended during the war and it was not till February 1920, that the Club really got together again.

At a meeting held during that month, under the Presidency of Sir Charles Higham, the first plans were made for the great Advertising Exhibition at the White City, which took place the next year under Sir (then Mr.) William Crawford's Presidency.

There had been other Advertising Exhibitions. The *Advertiser's Weekly* for instance sponsored one at the Holland Park Rink in October 1913. But none of them was so spectacular as the White City Exhibition in 1921. This Exhibition in large measure achieved its object in driving home to the public the benefits of advertising—and its importance as a factor in modern industry.

Three prominent features may be worth mentioning.

Firstly, it was honoured by probably the largest Royal Visit ever paid to any exhibition. King George the Fifth, Queen Mary, Queen Alexandra, the King and Queen of Denmark, Princess Mary and the Queen of Norway and Princess Victoria all attended in one party.

The Committee all turned up in top hats and tails—after lessons in how to address Royalty—to show the distinguished guests round the exhibits. It fell to my lot to accompany Queen Alexandra. She, poor dear, was very deaf, and I still remember saying as we passed a particularly impressive stand, 'This, Madam, is the stand of the Carlton Studio', only to receive the bland remark, 'Oh! Does it?', to which I could think of no apt reply.

The next was the Lucky Dip, to which all sorts of manufacturers contributed branded goods to be distributed free. For the first day or two attendances were low despite excellent publicity in most of the papers. Then Northcliffe gave a main news page story in the *Daily Mail* with a heading of 'Thousands of Free Gifts at the White City'. From that day Wood Lane could not accommodate the queues.

The third was the Advertising Pageant which was run in connection with the Exhibition. It was something like the Lord Mayor's Show but few Lord Mayor's Shows have attracted such throngs to line the route.

A slightly less important Exhibition was organised by the Thirty Club at Olympia in 1933.

It was, incidentally, in connection with these exhibitions that the members of the Thirty Club suddenly realised that they were incurring heavy liabilities on an infinitesimal capital. So they not only increased their membership but became a Company limited by Guarantee.

The Aldwych

The Aldwych Club came into being, as I have mentioned, as the result of a suggestion by Wareham Smith, then Advertisement Director of Associated Newspapers, that the advertising business required some permanent meeting place.

The Thirty Club held an open dinner under the Presidency of George Orange in September 1910, when Wareham explained his plan, with the result that a few months later the Aldwych opened its doors at 18 Exeter Street where it still remains. It has never closed its doors except for a few days in 1915 when one of a string of Zeppelin bombs fell on the opposite pavement, brought in all the plate glass, cutting heavy leather settees in half and generally making an awful mess. I happened to be playing Auction in the lounge with Stanley Worth, a cousin of Stanley Baldwin, and two country members from Scarborough. As it sounded as if the Hun was sitting up on top trying to hit the Aldwych, I called out, 'Let's get to the cellar!', which we did only to find that what we thought was a cellar was actually a light-well and we were under the sky. We thought we got there quickly but we only beat the billiard marker from the fifth floor by a short head. All five of us hastily returned to the bar.

Three or four years later the four of us had a good laugh when a South African member, Cecil Sibbett, on a return visit to this country, solemnly presented the Club with a little glass case containing two pieces of twisted metal with the legend 'Portions of a Zeppelin bomb which fell outside the Aldwych Club and seriously disturbed a Bridge game. Presented by one of the players: Cecil J. Sibbett.'

The joke was that Sibbett had never been near the Club that night.

Evidently he had gone back to South Africa and told the story as you or I would have told it and, as we should have, came to believe it himself.

I, at least, learnt my lesson. Never adopt another man's story to yourself.

During the first World War, the Aldwych achieved considerable fame from the occasional luncheons it ran at the Connaught Rooms. The speakers included most of the leaders of the country, many of them speaking 'off the record'. Typical names in date order are: General Baden-Powell, Lord Northcliffe, Lord Derby, Sir Edward Carson, Lord Leverhulme, Winston Churchill (twice), Sir Auckland Geddes, J. H. Thomas, Lord Rhondda, Admiral Jellicoe, Bonar Law, J. R. Clynes and H. H. Asquith.

The choice of Asquith in June 1918, caused some comment. According to Philip Richardson, for long Hon. Secretary of the Club, 'Northcliffe House thundered against the lunch, said the Club would not get a Chairman and there would be very few present. Sir Albert Stanley, President of the Board of Trade, was our President at the time, but as a loyal supporter of Lloyd George he could not take the Chair. Others, including Lord Leverhulme, also refused and four days before the luncheon I went in desperation to see Asquith at the House of Commons and he suggested Lord Mersey. Thank goodness, this innocent old man accepted. There were over 700 present, including Mrs. Asquith in the gallery.'

Even for those functions, all of which were largely attended, 700 was quite an audience.

Its Presidents during this period included Wareham Smith, Lord Riddell, Sir Frank Newnes, Sir Hedley Le Bas, Gordon Selfridge, Lord Northcliffe and Lord Ashfield.

The Optimists

In dealing with this period one should not omit a reference to 'The Optimists'. This organisation, started by Charlie Higham, was very little concerned with advertising but it was responsible for the first prototype of the Home Guard of the second World War. Higham, almost on the outbreak of war in 1914, started 'The Optimists Corps', providing business-men who, for one reason or another—age, health, priority business, or what you will—could not enlist, with the chance of learning the rudiments of soldiering.

And it was the rudiments of war that he and our 'Colonel', John Manley of Hudson and Kearns, the printers, taught us. Many of us, not very long after, found our training very useful.

Later on, the Optimists were incorporated in the subsequent officially formed, organisation called the L.D.V. (Local Defence Volunteers), but it was an advertising man who sowed the seeds, Charlie Higham.

The Fleet Street

In talking of this era one must not ignore the Fleet Street Club, one of the earliest conceptions, possibly antedating the Sphinx. Membership of the Fleet Street was confined to representatives of the Press. Every day members would meet for lunch at the old Anderton's Hotel. They would exchange news as to the orders they had secured, discuss their day-to-day problems of whether to give so-and-so credit, whether it was worth cutting rates to the extent that Mr. X demanded and all the other troubles that affected an Advertisement Manager in those days. In some degrees they still do.

Once a year they held a dinner to entertain their friends and clients.

In November 1907, for example, it took place at the long forgotten Inns of Court Hotel. The *Advertising World* listed nearly one hundred guests, including on the Press side J. W. Cunnison (*Dundee Advertiser*) in the Chair, H. C. Anning (*Bristol Times & Mirror*), E. W. Barney (*London Opinion*), S. G. Coram (*Pearsons*), G. A. Godley (*Daily Mirror*), T. McAusland (*Pearsons*), A. Richardson (*Lloyd's News*), J. H. Salt (*T.P.'s Weekly*), F. C. Beveridge (*Belfast Telegraph*), A. H. Clackson (*The Guardian*), J. Duncan (*Birmingham Post*), A. E. Hodges (*Family Herald*), A. E. Hobbs (*Standard*), H. J. Lee (*Scotsman*), R. J. Owen (*North Mail*), E. Sothcott (*Lady's World*) and G. Wetton (*Daily Express*).

On the clients' side there were: G. Bashforth (Potter's), T. C. Bench (Smith's), F. E. Bennett, A. Burbridge, L. D. Falk (Keymer's), A. Goodall (Spottiswoode, Dixon & Hunting), A Goodale (Mather & Crowther), A. Harrison (Street's), L. Philips (Sell's), J. Strong (Mitchells), A. G. Spence (Muller's), A. G. Steele (Gordon & Gotch), A. H. Wells (Benson's) and a lot of others, including me.

Later on the Fleet Street broadened its membership and took its own premises in Cursitor Street. Its germ still exists in the Fleet Street-Column Club.

The Publicity

The only other London club that started before the first World War was the Publicity Club. The idea of the Club is said to have been conceived in a casual conversation at Marcus Heber Smith's Norfolk Studio in February 1913, and took final form at a meeting at Anderton's Hotel on March the 4th. The name of the Publicity Club of London was formally adopted. J. J. ('Jack') O'Neill was elected President, while other officers included H. Val Fisher (Editor of the *Advertising World*), A. J. Greenly, Eric Warne, Oscar Stanton, Roy Hazard, W. W. J. Studd and M. F. Travers Cleaver.

In January 1914, Andrew Milne took on the Honorary Secretaryship 'pro tem'. The 'pro tem' position lasted for ten years!

To commence with, the Club catered mainly for the younger generation of advertising men, women being inadmissible because at that time there were not enough women in the advertising business. Women were, in fact, not admitted till after the first World War and then by the narrow majority of one vote.

Almost from its start in 1913 the 'Pub. Club' has grown in influence and in membership.

Commencing with twenty-six members its membership grew steadily until the war forced it to suspend activities in March 1917. When it came to life again in November 1919, under the Chairmanship of W. M. Young, Jnr., the membership was ninety-five. Two months later it was 150. By October it was 280.

Meanwhile, the Publicity Club had played its part in building up the structure of Advertising in Great Britain. Many of its members, like those of the Thirty Club, had toured the provinces to form local clubs. Quite a number took part in the delegation to America and worked hard to secure delegates from that country.

Andrew Milne played as big a part as anybody in that historic adventure.

The Publicity Club is, by the way, the only Club with anything approaching a real record of its progress. If anybody wants to read the 'Fiery Torch' oration of Bill Crawford at the Club's revival meeting in November 1919, I believe the Club's records would provide it.

Meanwhile, over all the years the Publicity Club of London has grown and flourished. At the time of writing, forty years after its foundation, its membership is well over 700.

The Regent

It was ten years later that the next London Advertising Club was started. This was the Regent. For some time Cyril Freer had been giving a series of lectures on Advertising at the London Polytechnic. In May 1923, some of his students held a meeting at the Caxton Hall and formed the Regent Advertising Club. Cyril Freer was elected Chairman and Mrs. Ethel M. Wood, C.B.E., Vice-chairman.

Designed primarily to help the younger generation of advertising men and women, the Club made rapid progress and over 120 members registered as delegates for the Exhibition and Convention at Olympia in 1927.

The next year it opened its own premises at 19 Buckingham Street, Strand, whence after the second World War it finally moved to Chesterfield Street in Mayfair.

The Women

Two or three months after the Regent started another and very significant body came into being—the Women's Advertising Club of London.

There had been a previous attempt at starting a Women's Club in 1909 or 1910 under the title of the Association of Advertising Women. Miss J. A. Reynolds of Samson Clark & Co. and Miss Johnson of the London Shoe Co. were the two ladies who were its main inspiration with Miss Sayer of A. J. Wilson & Co., who became its first President.

Other original members were Miss Marion Jean Lyon of *Punch*, Mrs. Mortimer of the *Daily Mirror*, Miss Spriggs of Spriggs Agency, Miss Parker of Pitman's and Miss Hietland of Evans Bros.

In 1914 it had grown sufficiently to have a stand at the International Advertising Exhibition at Holland Park Hall.

The Association was dissolved during the first World War but in the early days of that war the members, with the aid of the Taxi Owners Association, organised mass trips for wounded soldiers to places of interest in the countryside.

In establishing the still flourishing Women's Advertising Club of London in 1923, the Thirty Club again played a big part. With the 1924 Convention impending three members of the '30', John Cheshire, Harold Vernon and Bill Crawford, decided to try to get our advertising women together to act as hostesses to the American women.

So successful were they that they subsequently came to be called the 'Godfathers' of the Women's Advertising Club of London.

The first President was Marion Jean Lyon, who after serving an apprenticeship with Derricks, went to *Punch* as assistant to Roy Somerville. Roy was a very able advertising man but he was a complete cripple and Marion Lyon had to act as his right arm and his legs. Between them they transformed *Punch* from a completely ignored advertising medium selling at £25 a page to the *Punch* that we know today.

Eventually Marion Lyon married Raven Hill, the famous artist.

It may have been out of gratitude to the Club's 'Godfathers' that in December 1924, while I was President of the '30', the Women's Club under the Presidency of Mrs. A. J. Wilson entertained the members of the Thirty Club to a dinner-dance at the old Prince's Restaurant.

If the *Advertiser's Weekly* is correct, Mrs. Wilson made a brilliant speech and I made a more or less adequate response.

At any rate a good time was had by all.

And lastly Golf

Although it has always called itself a 'Society', I think the Newspaper and Advertising Golfing Society, commonly known as N.A.G.S., really falls within the scope of this chapter.

The Advertisers Golfing Society, as was its original name, played its first match on 6th November 1907, when according to the *Advertising World*, it defeated the London Press Golfing Society by 8¼ points to 3¾ points.

The teams for this historic encounter were:

A.G.S.: F. H. Newnes, M.P., Brame Hillyard, A. Tindall Atkinson, C. S. Cox, H. E. Morgan, H. F. Le Bas, P. C. Burton, J. A. S. Mackie.

L.P.G.S.: A. J. Robertson, G. C. Smith, Emsley Carr, A. M. Faulkner, G. A. Riddell, S. J. Southerton, H. Leach, L. G. Taylor.

It is interesting to note that at least five of the players, Newnes, Morgan, Le Bas, Emsley Carr and, of course, the then 'Mr.' Riddell, subsequently attained titles.

H. E. Morgan was the first Hon. Secretary.

And the N.A.G.S. still flourishes.

The Provincial Clubs

Members of the Provincial Clubs must forgive me for not having been able to treat their Clubs in detail but *Who's Who in British Advertising* for 1924 records the following towns as having Publicity Clubs: Bradford, Edinburgh, Glasgow, Hull, Leeds, Liverpool, Manchester, Newcastle and Oxford.

Except for the Newcastle Club, which was called The Advertising Club of Newcastle, all of these were called 'The Publicity Club' of the town concerned.

There were also in existence The Publicity Club of Ireland and The Advertising Club of Ulster.

5. The World's First International Advertising Convention

AFTER THE success of its White City Exhibition, the Thirty Club revived one of its pre-war ambitions.

For many years the annual conventions of the American Advertising Clubs had ranked high among the conventions of which Americans were and still are so fond.

Individual members of British Clubs had visited these conventions and reported on them enthusiastically. The Publicity Club's records show that in 1913 they commissioned a banner bearing the Club's device, which Percy Burton presented at the Baltimore Convention.

When the Association changed its name to the Associated Advertising Clubs of the World (A.A.C.W.), the Thirty Club of London became its first overseas member.

The '30's' greatest desire was to persuade the A.A.C.W. to hold one of its conventions in London and in 1922 the '30' sent a small delegation under Sir Charles Higham to the Milwaukee Convention to invite the Americans to hold their 1924 Convention in London. (Before the war it had sent an official delegation to Houston, Texas.)

Higham's invitation received sufficient support for the Club to decide to send a really strong delegation to Philadelphia the next year (1923) to fight for the 1924 Convention.

The result was that on 26 May 1923 a delegation of 116 British advertising men and women, led by John Cheshire of Lever's, then President of the Club, set sail on the

Berengaria, a one-time German liner taken over by the Cunard as part of the British reparations under the Peace Treaty.

A night or two before we sailed, the delegates were given a large dinner under the Chairmanship of Sir William Berry (later Lord Camrose). Of his speech I well remember one of his lighter stories. As a young man, he said, he was called on to speak at a dinner of the New York Advertising Club. In the course of his speech he told three of the newest and best stories out of his wide repertoire. When he sat down, the Toastmaster, who in the States is a member and not a paid official in a red coat, got up and in thanking 'their young friend from England' ended by saying: 'We are particularly pleased to know that three of our oldest and best stories have at last reached that Country.'

Some of us took the story to heart and, in the speeches we had to make in the States in our campaign, studiously avoided trying to tell funny stories. The only one I ever used was Bill Berry's own and I found it went down very well as a closing apology for not having followed the common U.S. practice.

May the 26th, 1923, was a typically lovely day. We mustered at Waterloo and went down by the 12.10 Boat Train. Once on the *Berengaria*, we sorted ourselves out, found our cabins and explored the ship. For most of us, including myself, it was our first knowledge of a ship of that size. My nearest was the perhaps 3,000-ton *Prinz Regent Luitpold* on which the family had come to England in 1897.

I still remember my appreciation of a then recent cartoon by Watts in the *Sketch*, showing an insignificant little man at the bottom of two imposing lifts, plaintively asking a steward: 'Say, Steward, can you tell me the way to the sea?' I felt in need of the same information.

Anyway most of us did know that dressing for dinner on the first night was not 'done' and it gave me a bit of a shock to see two very distinguished delegates, who shall be nameless, parading the deck that night in full evening dress and wearing opera hats.

The next afternoon Cheshire and Harold Vernon, next year's President-to-be, aided by Andrew Milne, who more or less acted as our Manager, got us together and gave us the outline of our campaign to capture the 1924 Convention. Other meetings small and large took place every day.

I don't think anyone has a complete list of the delegates but the following names may ring a bell in some of the older memories. They are in alphabetical order and if some of the initials are missing, it is because my notes of the period are faulty.

Some of the Delegates to Philadelphia

Agnew, E. S.
Akerman, J. C.
Allen, J.
Allison, J. Murray
Baird, Sir Robert
Bates, C. Arthur
Bennett, F.
Boys, A.
Bradley, H. B.
Bradshaw, Percy
Brinninkmeyer, —
Broughton, H. H.
Bruce, Robert
Chadwick, Arthur
Cheshire, John
Clark, Roy
Clark, Samson
Cooper, —
Crawford, W. S.
Day, W. T.
Derry, Frank
Derwent, H. C.
Derwent, W. R.
Dunkley, W. H.
Durham, T. C.
Emanuel, Philip
Evans, H. S.
Falk, L. D.
Field, Eric
Field, Harry
Fitch, H. Rae
Fraser, Ivor
Girardot, E. D.
Greenly, A. J.
Harwood, Leslie
Haines, R.
Henderson, J. S.
Houghton, Sam
Hutchings, R. W.
Hutchinson, Lt.-Col.
Illingworth, E. N.
Imber, Horace
Jauncey, W. L.
Johnston, Fred
Kelly, H. M.
Lawson, Lt.-Col. F. F.
MacLachlan, Miss W. S.
Marrian, W. L.
Mascord, G. W.
McDougall, Thomas
McNab, W. J.
Meaker, E. J.
Milne, Andrew
Mitchell, J. C.
Montford, C.
Morgans, E. J.
Morison, Ernest
Morris, Herbert
Mumford, —
Napier, F. C.
Neaverson, H.
O'Keefe, W.
Popper, D. H.
Porter, A. S.
Potter, F. E.
Pritchard, Fleetwood
Ridout, H. C.
Roberts, A. C.
Robertson, E. J.
Rossiter, A. J.
Rowe, B. W.
Rozier, A. W.
Savage, Major J. C.
Scott, George
Shoesmith, Fred
Smith, P. G. A.
Spicer, R. E.
Steinberg, Louis
Stembridge, G.
Talcott, Wally
Taylor, A. J.
Thornberry, Robert
Tolley, —
Vernon, Harold
Vernon, Leslie C.
Walker, E. T.
Wallace, W. T.
Walley, Thomas
Walmsley, U. B.
Watts, A. K.
Webb, W. H.
Wells, H. M.
Westenholme, —

In addition many delegates brought their wives to add beauty and charm to help the campaign.

For all of us it was a memorable voyage but Fleetwood Pritchard has a special reason to be glad he made the trip. Thanks to drawing a lucky number in the daily pool, he was able to stay in the States a fortnight longer than he had planned. During that fortnight he met the gracious lady who has given him so many happy years of married life.

Except for one day the weather throughout the trip was perfect and for most of us, with something to do all day and every day, it passed all too quickly.

In the afternoon of 1 June we stopped at Quarantine and a few of us, who got through the formalities quickly, were able to leave the ship and get on the tender to Manhattan Island.

By doing so we missed something of the famous and never-to-be forgotten 'skyline' but we did reach the Hotel Pennsylvania ahead of the crowd with time to have a bath in preparation for the enormous banquet which awaited us. Full dress was forbidden for all through the delay of the ship.

Lack of formality in dress did not prevent the banquet that was waiting for us being quite overwhelming. When the Americans really lay themselves out on this sort of thing, they certainly do it well.

As regards our campaign, it was very obvious that the New York delegation to Atlantic City was already 'sold' on the idea of 'London, 1924'.

This fact being established, we had no reason to delay in New York and after a very enjoyable week-end at the Westchester Biltmore Country Club, off we went to Atlantic City, the super, super Brighton where the Convention was being held.

One's first view of the towering skyscrapers of hotels lining the famous 'Board Walk' was something new to us. So was the luxury of the hotels in which we stayed.

Here, except for those of us scheduled to speak at the Convention, our main work was personal 'lobbying', at which some of our members were so successful that when the voting came there was no doubt that 'London, 1924' it was.

Then the second part of our work began. It was to visit the clubs in the big cities and try to secure as big delegations as possible. In a spirit of optimism dates had already been arranged for those of us who could stay a little longer in the States, so that roughly we could cover the country. I do not remember the assignment of other delegates but I know that I spoke at Philadelphia, Pittsburgh, Cincinnatti, Chicago, Kansas City, Milwaukee and Buffalo.

Everywhere we received a wonderful welcome and it was obvious that the idea of coming over to 'the old country' was an inspiring thought to our very large audiences.

When we got back to England, we had to get down to brass tacks and get busy organising what we had decided should be the first really International Advertising Convention in the world. To promote this object the A.A.C.W. had established a new District: District 14, to include all the world outside America and Canada. Harold Vernon became its first Chairman. As such we had to rope in not only all the Continental countries but other overseas countries as well.

The task was not an easy one and it was not made any easier by a speech by Charlie Higham, who had played such a vital part in the early stages, to the Publicity Club in October 1923.

It may be worth quoting some of his speech as it was reported in the *Advertiser's Weekly* of 5 October 1923.

'He was very much worried as to what sort of convention was going to be held in England. He was a member of the Thirty Club and visited America for the purpose of inviting the Convention to England. At Milwaukee he spoke thirty-seven times in fifteen days and on his return it was four months before the Thirty Club gave him the honour of listening to him as to what had happened.

'The Thirty Club undertook the responsibility of the Convention when they issued the invitation and he regretted that a month ago they decided to leave the organising to

District 14 of the A.A.C.W. . . . and our American visitors at the present moment had no hopes. Money was in the hands of one Club, when it should be in the hands of many. It had been well spent and well directed. However, they must know where they were.

'He did not want the Convention held at Wembley. He had already suggested the Central Hall, Westminster. . . . He thought there was enough influence in that room to bring pressure on the Thirty Club to call together all the interests of advertising and discuss ways and means; to tell how much money was being spent and how much was in hand.

'He wanted the Chairman and members of every Committee to resign and offer themselves for re-election at that large conference.

' "I do not propose," he concluded, "to stand at the back of three or four men and do the work until July the 12th and then step in the background and let them take the glory." '

(Just imagine Charlie Higham ever doing that!)

Despite Higham's oratory, and I still think he was the only orator in the real sense of the word that we have ever had in the business, the result was a unanimous vote pledging the Publicity to support the Thirty Club in its work for 1924.

And, in fact, all the important steps that Higham wanted had already been taken, with the one exception of holding the Convention itself at the Central Hall, Westminster.

Subsequent events proved just how wrong he was.

We had already roped in officers of all the Clubs; we had worked out what Committees were needed, had found among the Clubs the most suitable Chairmen, given them their terms of reference and left them to find the best members they could.

Above them all was the Central Committee under the Chairmanship of Harold Vernon.

As for finance, we were assured of nearly £50,000 and when it was all over a percentage was returned to the subscribers and, with their consent, enough retained to provide the initial finance for the Advertising Association.

I found myself Chairman of the Overseas Committee, charged with securing delegations from all countries outside the U.S. and Canada, providing for their hospitality and finding places for them on the programme.

In this work I found a wonderful adjutant in Fernand Marteau. When July arrived we had whipped up delegations from France, Holland, Belgium, Spain, Italy, Sweden, Denmark, Norway, Latin-America, India, Japan, China and South Africa.

Meanwhile, the Americans had been busy. Enrolments were so heavy that they decided to charter two ships for the main body of delegates, certainly the first and possibly the only private charter of liners to cross the Atlantic. One was a U.S. boat, the *Republic*; the other a Cunarder, the *Lancastria* which was subsequently to be so tragically bombed at St. Nazaire in 1940.

They asked the Thirty Club to send two men to act as liaison officers. I was lucky enough to be one. A. H. ('Billy') Williams of Selfridges was the other.

After a very dull trip on the *Majestic* at the Commodore's table, we had a couple of hectic days in New York and set sail for home.

Being slightly the senior, I was posted to the *Republic* as it was the H.Q. Ship. Being a U.S. liner, it was a 'dry' boat —Bill's wasn't!

Despite that, I had a wonderfully interesting trip. Every morning at 10 I would be in the Smoke Room answering personal questions. Everybody on board had had ancestors in England. Where was Wigan? What sort of a town was it? Had it really got a pier? How far was Stockport from London? You can imagine the sort of things they wanted to know and you can imagine how grateful I was to one ex-Englishman among the delegates who gave me a copy of the *A.B.C. Timetable*. I had never realised what a fund of knowledge that book could provide.

After lunch I would talk for an hour to an enthralled audience about what they were going to see and to do. I worked out a diagrammatic map of London on which Piccadilly and the Strand were roughly a straight line, slowly converging at the Bank with another straight line consisting of Oxford Street, Holborn and Cheapside.

I had also secured enough English coins to show them on a board alongside their nearest U.S. counterparts.

Anything of this sort interested the delegates immensely.

What with this kind of occupation and conferences with the A.A.C.W. Committee, I was pretty well dead when we eventually reached Southampton.

I still remember one terribly serious conference. The delegates from the Poor Richard Club had brought with them a couple of gavels made out of oak from the original Hall of Independence. They were much afraid that we in England might still be resentful of the loss of such an important colony. I think I was right in reassuring them on this point.

But at the end of the voyage I had my greatest thrill of all.

Being on a direct charter, we did not follow the usual liner's route via Cherbourg and then to Southampton by the eastern side of the Isle of Wight. Instead, after passing Bishop Rock, we hugged the English coast all the way up to the Needles and left the Isle of Wight on our starboard bow.

It was a wonderful day and the lovely green of England was something the Americans had never seen.

As the lone Englishman on the boat I got a tremendous kick out of their enthusiasm.

At Southampton the delegates were welcomed by a Reception Committee consisting of, among others, the Mayor and Mayoress of Southampton, John Cheshire, Harold Vernon, Sir Charles Higham, W. S. Crawford, Sir Herbert Morgan, the Rt. Hon. G. H. Roberts, P.C., Horace Imber and F. Van den Hueval.

Writing at this date, it seems ironic that Lou Holland, President of the A.A.C.W. and Head of the U.S. Delegation, should say about the Convention, 'I hope it will be the forerunner of that world peace we all so much desire.'

At Waterloo a similar reception awaited the delegates. Thence they were taken to their hotels to finish a wonderful day with an even more wonderful function at the Albert Hall.

And then the Convention itself.

My main part in the Convention was looking after the Continental and other overseas delegates and conducting the Export Sessions.

On the Wednesday we gave a dinner at the Piccadilly Hotel to the French-speaking delegates. As Chairman I had an unexpected privilege, that of introducing M. Herriot, the Prime Minister of France, who on his first public appearance in England replied to the toast of *La Belle France*, proposed by me in my very best French. Once more I quote, this time from M. Herriot: 'Great Britain, that great country, which they greeted as the historic protector, which she will always be, of Truth, Justice and Liberty.' I can only hope that the French still feel the same way.

Other speakers were Etienne Damour, President of the French Society of Advertising Agents, Charles Maillard, President of the Federation of French Publicity, Senator Paul Dupuy, Director of *Le Petit Parisien*, representatives of Belgium and Switzerland and our own Fernand Marteau and John Hart.

This function received a surprising amount of publicity, including for some unknown reason three-quarters of a column in the *Madras Mail*.

The opening of the Convention by H.R.H. the Prince of Wales and the great success of the Convention I will leave to other people's pens.

With one offshoot of the Convention only I can deal. The A.A.C.W. had been invited by the French authorities to send a delegation to Paris when the Wembley functions were over.

The A.A.C.W. paid me the compliment of asking me to organise and to lead the delegation to Paris.

So on Saturday, the 26th of July, 500 Americans led by Jesse H. Neal and accompanied by Vernon, Crawford,

John Hart, MacDougall, Roy Clark, McCarther and me proceeded to Paris.

At Calais, the *Gare Maritime* was *en fête* and the Civic authorities were waiting to welcome us with champagne and speeches.

When our special train reached the *Gare du Nord*, we found it bedecked with flags and bunting in honour of the occasion and crowded with Parisians to add their unofficial greeting to the visitors.

The next morning we were driven to the *Arc de Triomphe* for Jesse Neal to lay a bronze palm on the grave of the Unknown Warrior, while the guard of honour presented arms and the band of the 31st Infantry Regiment played the American and French National Anthems.

In the afternoon the party journeyed to Versailles to hear more speeches and be conducted round the Palace.

At night dinner was served in the *Trianon*, the first time this historic spot had ever been employed for such a function.

Immediately after the banquet the party motored to the Terrace of Fountains to view a specially devised firework display, a reproduction of a famous display during the reign of Louis XIV.

The scene with the fireworks reflected in the lakes was one of unforgettable beauty.

The Monday was also a busy day. It opened with a reception by the Municipality at the *Hotel de Ville*, where the Minister of Commerce supported by other officials expressed the Government's welcome. H. H. Charles, President of the Advertising Club of New York, responded and Jarvis Wood of the Poor Richard Club presented to the city one of the gavels from the Hall of Independence.

Next came a reception and lunch by the American Chamber of Commerce, attended by the American Ambassador.

In the afternoon came what was probably the most keenly appreciated compliment to the visitors—a reception by the President of the Republic (M. Gaston Doumergue) at the

Elysée Palace. The approaches to the Palace were lined with a guard of honour of the Republican Guard.

The day closed with a banquet at the Hotel Continental at which the Government was represented by M. Chautemps, Minister of the Interior, who decorated Jesse Neal and Charles with the Legion of Honour.

On the Tuesday, after a visit to the Agence Havas, the delegates were taken to Le Bourget for a special demonstration of trick flying.

The last function of all was a gala performance at the Opera. Here the magnificent staircase was lined by a guard of honour of the famous Chasseurs. During the entracte the delegates presented their hosts with a bust of Benjamin Franklin.

It was a worthy climax to a wonderful week-end and a wonderful Convention.

6. How the Newspapers Woke Up

IT WAS about the turn of the century that the newspapers first began to realise just what advertising could mean to them.

Even Northcliffe's launching of the *Daily Mail* on 4 May 1896, disturbing as his competitors found it, did not have much of an impact on their attitude to advertising.

At that time very few newspapers accepted display type or blocks. The 1895 issue of *Successful Advertising*, an annual directory published by Smith's Advertising Agency, mentions that the *Daily News* 'has the distinctive feature of allowing bold type and double column advertisements. It also inserts blocks.' The *Daily Graphic* would insert blocks on one page, while the *Echo* conceded double column advertisements but jibbed at blocks. As for the *Morning Post*, it was not to accept anything over Single Columns till 1910.

Alfred Harmsworth himself, genius that he was, does not seem to have envisaged the possibilities of advertising. Like all its contemporaries, the front page of the *Mail* was confined entirely to 'smalls' and the public had to wait six years to see an advertisement occupy the whole front page, one of Mellin's Food on Coronation Day, 11 August 1902.

In the first issue the only displayed advertisements in the whole of the eight-page paper were on the back page and consisted of a Double Column of Dr. Tibbles Vi-Cocoa, a half-Double of Bovril, a 6-inch Double Column of Erard Pianos, a 1½-inch Double Column of Harris' Sewing Machines and a 4-inch Single Column of Krog's Malted

Food for Horses. The only advertisements to carry an illustration were the last two.

Otherwise the only 'display' was by means of 'drop letters'. Altogether out of the fifty-six columns in the paper sixteen and a half were occupied by advertising.

It was, in fact, not till 1900 that the Chief allowed display type to be used on the front page at all and then only for Publishers and only below 'the fold'.

This revolutionary development was not due to Northcliffe's initiative. The credit must go to Wareham Smith, then in charge of the advertising department at a salary of a few pounds a week.

Thirty years later, Wareham wrote an autobiography under the title of *Spilt Ink*, published by Ernest Benn Ltd. The book is out of print and I cannot think of any greater tribute to my old friend than to quote his own story of how it all happened and the difficulties he had to overcome.

Wareham, I should mention, had had his first connection with the newspaper business when as a boy of eleven, while still at school, he delivered newspapers in the mornings and sold them on the streets in the evenings.

Now I start quoting.

'The newspaper trade has changed materially since then—1885—and so also have the conditions of labour. In those days machines did not fold newspapers. You went at four or five in the morning to your wholesaler, somewhere off Fleet Street—to whom, by the way, you were generally in debt—a heavy bundle of unfolded papers was thrown at you, and you brought it back to your shop as best you could. Then it was all hands on deck—my boss, by name Saunders, his wife, two daughters and myself—to fold. One of the daughters was a very pretty girl. I fell madly in love with her. She was sixteen. The work of folding was hard until the knack was acquired, and for a time I went out with sore fingers.

'My day's time-table was as follows: Six a.m. at the shop. Seven to eight delivering papers—a snatched breakfast.

School, nine to twelve and a look-in at the shop to do odd jobs. School again in the afternoon from two to four-thirty. Then shop again for a cup of tea and bread and dripping—which I loathed, having been largely brought up on it. After tea I helped to fold evening papers and then took them out to sell. Home about nine, and so to bed.

'I shall always remember the dreadful agony of getting myself out of bed in the mornings, Sundays included, in the early days of that job. The Sunday paper round took three hours. My mother tried to make me give up the work, but curiously enough I took to it kindly. And, besides, I needed the money—half a crown a week and a small (very small) commission. From earliest recollection I was always "finicky" about clothes, and I was allowed to keep my earnings for sartorial purposes.

'About this time I had a very useful lesson in commercial morality. Customers for penny papers, such as the *Standard*, were scarce, and it was the ambition of every newsboy to get hold of a "penny" client. My rival—a great, hulking brute, as I remember him—had one. One night I happened to get there first and I planted my *Standard*. The customer asked where his usual boy was. I said he was ill.

'I had good reason to find out that he was by no means ill or weak. As soon as he learned what had happened, he gave me the biggest hiding I have ever received. I never forgot it. Truth is safer than fiction!

'It is far from my wish to give the impression that I regarded my life in those, alas, far bygone days as hard. I didn't, and I don't now. The law, in its wisdom, does not permit these conditions today. But, thank heaven, I was born before the law took to dry-nursing. I learned how to work and acquired the habit. I also acquired a spirit of independence and self-reliance. I do not find a superabundance of this kind of thing in the modern youth. But that may be because my circle of youthful acquaintances is limited.'

Wareham's first actual job in a newspaper office was in

1890 when he became office boy to John Cowley, then advertisement clerk of the *Evening News*.

Dismissed from that job for some reason which he does not mention, Wareham worked for two firms of solicitors until the advent of the *Mail*. Answering an advertisement in the paper, he became a clerk in the advertising department at twenty-five shillings a week.

'To my surprise', he writes, 'on arrival at the *Daily Mail* (the offices then were at 2 Carmelite Street) I found my old friend Lingard installed as general manager. My two other old acquaintances, John Cowley and H. W. Whittingham, were respectively manager and advertisement manager of the *Evening News*. The chief advertisement clerk was A. J. Wall, now, for many years past, London manager of the *Irish Independent*. I was his assistant, and there was another clerk named Hayward (still with the *Daily Mirror*). There were three outside representatives, Gilbert A. Godley, Gould and Lancaster.

'I found things had not materially altered since I had left the *Evening News* six years before. As regards press advertising, it was still practically non-existent, judged in the light of modern achievements. Nearly every newspaper specialised in "classified" advertisements, the *Daily Telegraph*, *Daily Chronicle* and *Daily News* having almost a monopoly. There was little or no advertising of big stores, book publishers, railways, finance, resorts and a host of others that in recent years have been so prominently before the public.

'Most papers would not admit display or illustrated advertisements, and advertisers themselves objected to them.

'The newspaper-office routine was crude. The advertisement manager, or chief advertisement clerk—they were mostly clerks—started work by seeing what advertisements other newspapers had printed which were not in his own publication. Then he would cut them out and hand them to the canvassing staff for "necessary action". There was no attempt at creating advertising. The initiative, such as existed was still in the advertiser's office.

'In the *Daily Mail* office things were pretty much the same as in any business office. They were the days of silk hats, frock coats and patent-leather boots. Representative and manager usually came to the office in striped trousers and lounge-coat and vest. You kept your silk hat, frock coat, etc., in a cupboard and changed on your arrival.

'It was the custom for representatives and managers to meet at Street's Advertising Agency in Cornhill, E.C., at four p.m. and gather information as to what advertising was being given out and by whom. Then you had a drink or two at a hostelry near by and strolled round to put the usual questions, hoping to get an order.

'A story is told that one day a principal of Street's was passing through the general office and overheard a representative ask:

' "Anything for me today?" The principal said to the reception clerk: "I have seen that man many times. Who is he?"

' "I don't know."

' "What's his name?"

' "I don't know."

' "What paper does he represent?"

' "I don't know. He has been coming here for years and even now I don't know his name or the name of his paper, and I have, of course, never given him an order."

'So we went on for two or three years during which time Wall fell ill and I took over his job, as I had planned—although, of course, I had not planned his illness! But I was ready and had made myself solid with Lingard. Meanwhile a new building had been erected, called Harmsworth Buildings—later to be known as Carmelite House—and when we moved in I was, to all intents and purposes, advertisement manager of the *Daily Mail*, at, I think, £3 a week.

'Advertisements were coming in more freely—be it said, of their own volition—but the paper remained in appearance and size the same as it was in its first issue.

'Then, in about the year 1900, or maybe a little earlier,

Alfred sat up in his chair and took a little notice of the advertisement department. Alfred discovered *me*. I had seen little of him up till then. One afternoon a phone message summoned me to his room. He was reclining in his favourite chair. (I never once, in twenty-five years, saw him working at his desk.)

' "Your name is Smith, isn't it?"

' "Yes, sir."

' "You are in charge of the advertisement department?"

' "Yes, sir."

' "When are you going to start thinking? When are you going to *do* something? The advertisement columns all look alike. They are the same today as in the first issue. I want to see something different. Start thinking. I'm busy now. Good day."

'That interview altered my whole outlook on life, and, incidentally, it was the genesis of press advertising as we know it today.

'If Alfred had not been the man he was, the result of that interview might have been disastrous to me. I did start to think. I lay awake thinking for hours during the next few nights. And then I went to Harmsworth with the suggestion that if he let me put "display" type on the front page, which, up to that date, was in appearance like the front page of *The Times*, I would get more publishers' announcements. I also had in view many other channels of advertising revenue if I could get permission to use display type. But I did not disclose my plans at the time.

'Alfred said: "I don't object. But the display type must be kept under the 'fold'. (The 'fold' is half-way down the page.) Submit specimens to me."

'The immediate result was that, one morning, the paper came out with the publishers' announcements set in display type on the front page. On my arrival at the office Lingard, whom I had not consulted, asked for an explanation. I told him what had happened and it made him furious. I must go through him. I was not to go to Sir Alfred. He had a great liking for me, but if anything of the sort occurred again we should have to part.

'I did not see how I was to continue "thinking" under these conditions, so I reported the matter to Sir Alfred. Alfred said: "I like the start. Get on with your job and leave Lingard to me."

'Nothing more on this subject did I hear from Lingard again. I handled him diplomatically, and, to his eternal credit, he showed no signs afterwards of any ill-will.

'In the course of time I filled the lower half of the front page every Friday with publishers' advertisements set in display type, and then I tackled Alfred again. I wanted the whole of the front page for display and illustrations this time, and I promised him drapers (now known as stores), railways, and all sorts of revenue-producing things.

'Alfred protested. Publishers were high-class advertisers. How did he know that I would not vulgarise—a favourite word of his in regard to advertising—the paper if he extended the privilege? However, he eventually agreed to my having display type on the entire page on Mondays and Fridays, but with no illustration.

'But from the time he gave me permission for the greater use of display type the Chief was never happy about it. The type was a constant irritation to him. I think he realised the importance of the work I was doing, but "type" offended him. And yet he plastered the sides of houses and railway bridges and the sky with hideous advertisements of the *Daily Mail*. He hated it, however, in his newspapers.

'The actual fight I had with him for illustrations and a wider range of type for advertisements—which was virtually a fight for the birth of modern press advertising—lasted for about three years, but the wounds resulting from it never healed. They were not allowed to. Week in and week out for years the advertisement department was in trouble with either the editor or the proprietor. Usually it was the size of the type. When it was not the type it was the illustrations. The type was too "overwhelming"—"bludgeoning" as the Chief called it—or the illustrations were too black, or the block didn't print well, or a bit of it showed through on the next page and gave a society woman a moustache.

'I allowed my arrangement regarding filling the lower half of the front page to continue for some time, and then I decided to tackle Alfred again. The result of the next interview was that I got a concession for illustrations under the fold and later over the whole page, and finally over the whole paper—and on every day of the week.

'This was a new departure in London daily newspaper advertising, and I think I am justified in claiming that it provided a tremendous lever which brought into existence many new classes of publicity. It certainly increased the yearly revenue of all newspapers throughout the country, apart from the *Daily Mail*, many hundreds of thousands of by pounds. The innovation enabled me to explore possibilities of revenue hitherto undreamed of.

'But it was certainly a fight to get things going. The more enterprise I showed the deeper I got into trouble.

'Still, I was allowed to go on, and when my pioneer work was beginning to show results, I got permission to increase the size of the paper to ten pages. A "dummy" was made up and I submitted it to the Chief.

'The ten-page paper ran for a day or two when I received the following wire from Paris: "Disgraceful make-up have asked Mr. Harold to stop ten-page paper you deliberately misled me. HARMSWORTH." '

Wareham had to survive this sort of thing till his retirement in 1921. He was not, of course, the only member of the staff to suffer from Northcliffe's censures. No one of importance on any of his staffs was free from criticism in his communiqués, as I found to my cost at Printing House Square. Editors and printers were also victims but Wareham seems to have been the favourite target and it says a lot for him that he persisted in his innovations in the face of such discouragement from the very one who should have welcomed them with open arms.

Even when Northcliffe started the *Daily Mirror* in December 1903, as an illustrated paper specially for women, he forbade any illustrated advertisements.

Wareham also deserves the credit for two minor but significant developments in newspaper advertising.

For the first years of the century advertisers fought shy of two days in the week, Mondays and Saturdays. Their main objection to Mondays was because it was 'Wash Day' and housewives were too busy to look at the paper, while on Saturdays men went straight from office or works to watch football games.

The idea of a five day week had, of course, never been thought of.

To prevent papers being so thin on Mondays, Wareham started a real drive on the drapers with such success that he not only filled his papers with them on Mondays but made it difficult for other types of advertisers to get in on Tuesdays and Wednesdays.

Severe thinness on Saturdays persisted until January 1923, when the *Daily Mail* came out with a Double Column of 'Bargain Spaces', the idea of a clerk in the Advertisement Department called Louis Casseras.

Papers are still on the thin side on Saturdays, but where would they be without their Bargain pages?

One little idea of Wareham's may be worth mentioning.

Readers may remember how one of the big dailies recently hired one of the first officers to be 'axed' under the Defence Cuts and offered to lend him to any readers. The idea was not new. In 1909 the *Evening News* at Wareham's suggestion did exactly the same thing, though, of course, without any connection with 'demobbing'.

A man called Arthur Goode—actually his name was Charles Tranton—inserted a small in the *Mail* headed, 'Man for Sale'.

Quoting again from *Spilt Ink*:

'The advertisement appeared as follows:

' "A man for sale. A cheerful English business man,

having serious need of £200 before December 15, is prepared to place his entire services at the complete disposal of any person or company. For the space of twelve months he will do anything and everything to further the interests or the comfort of his employer. He is so intelligent and so original, so good-tempered and methodically energetic, that anyone securing his services will never regret their bargain. This can be guaranteed by a host of personal friends. Interviews are solicited or full particulars will be sent in writing by Mr. Arthur Goode, 8 Manchester Street, London, W."

'There was obviously a first-rate news story somewhere in this advertisement, and an *Evening News* reporter interviewed Mr. Goode in his boarding-house. The story got four inches of editorial space.

'Goode's advertisement, in one particular at least, was inaccurate. He had no friends. He was, in fact, in a most desperate position. But he was certainly versatile and had plenty of pluck and self-confidence—a happy mixture of Mark Tapley and Micawber.

'But his story stuck in the office, and negotiations were opened with him to become "Our Man" on the *Evening News*. The negotiations were successful. Four days after the advertisement appeared, a whole column on the front page announced that the paper had "bought a man"! His services were at the disposal of anybody for any kind of job for nothing.

'The announcement was a marvellous piece of characterisation of the impeccable Mr. Goode, it more than filled in the few gaps of his own fulsome advertisement. He was described as a "trained organiser, a well-read, well-schooled man of very pleasant manners, a bachelor several years under forty". As a matter of fact his appearance was by no means impressive; he was short and inclined to be stout; and it was not difficult to realise what he actually was—a grocer by trade.

'There is no doubt that the idea was bright from the

editorial point of view, but its very originality hampered it, for it was some days before there was a bite. In the meanwhile, columns appeared each day disclosing the marvellous capacity of Goode to do anything, from the complete reorganisation of the largest and most complicated business to acting as nursemaid. It was variously stated that he was capable of acting as waiter, a hotel-reception clerk, canvasser for parliamentary candidate (an election was in the offing), engaging servants, interviewing candidates for staff appointments, attending children's parties, care of children over four years of age, playing over new songs and music, visiting hospitals, assisting suffragettes, acting as coach to hockey teams, teaching anyone the rudiments of chess, bridge, letter-writing, advertisement writing, happiness.

'A fairly comprehensive list!

'He got his first job on 8th December. He was lent to the Women's Freedom League to assist in the decoration of the Albert Hall for one of their meetings. It is not recorded that he did very much, but he seemed to have created an impression, because the next few months provided him with a very busy life.

'People were not slow to realise that there was a certain amount of publicity, or notoriety, attaching to employing the *Evening News* "man", and he was much in demand for dinner-parties, presumably to assist in their organisation, but actually, I believe, as a kind of queer show-piece. He assisted to produce a pantomime and such-like affairs in search of cheap advertisement—roller-skating carnivals (then very popular) particularly.

'Goode's engagement with the *Evening News* was for six months. For the first two the scheme went merrily. But at the end of that time interest began to fade. It was not his fault. The novelty had worn off and the jobs forthcoming were not sufficiently outstanding to keep the news end going. "Our Man", as a feature of publicity, lost his usefulness from the paper's point of view.'

I can add one fact to Wareham's story of Arthur Goode.

Charles Tranton in a surprising fashion helped to establish the fact that advertising agents are, in Law, principals. In 1917 the case of Tranton *v.* Astor was heard by Mr. Justice Low.

Tranton as a Common Informer, sought to recover penalties under the House of Commons (Disqualifications) Acts from Astor, then proprietor of the *Observer*, for voting in the House while enjoying a Government contract.

The 'contract' was an order from the Caxton Advertising Agency for an advertisement for recruits.

Le Bas and I gave evidence that the order was placed by the Caxton as a principal and therefore Astor never had a contract with the Government at all. The Judge accepted this, saying:

'I entirely accept Sir Hedley Le Bas' evidence with regard to this and his customer's and the newspaper's relative positions . . . the only contracts made by the defendant are a series of contracts with the Caxton Advertising Agency and with no one else . . . there is no privity of contract between any Government department and the *Observer* newspaper.'

His judgment, however, for Astor was also affected by the fact that, as the *Observer* had never acknowledged the order, the contract commenced and finished with its insertion and appearance in the paper. As the *Observer* went to press late on Saturday night and appeared in the early hours of Sunday morning, Astor could not possibly have voted in the House during the life of the 'contract'.

7. The Associations, Institutes and Societies

The Billposters

THE FIRST association of firms concerned purely with advertising was that of the Billposters or 'Paper Hangers' as they originally called themselves.

The movement had been under way for some years before, in May 1861, the United Kingdom Bill Posters' Association held its first General Meeting. One of its main functions was to supply advertisers with information as to the facilities available in towns all over the country. For this purpose it issued a Directory giving the names and addresses of its members, the population of each town and, for some reason, the name and publishing date of the local newspapers.

The 1861 issue contained 220 entries, covering 178 towns. London had three entries, while Manchester had no less than ten separate billposters.

It was just about this date that Sheldon's of Leeds took a step which was the forerunner of the orderly business we now know. Up to then all posting was catch as catch can 'fly posting'. Sheldon's actually rented sites for themselves!

This, however, is by the way and outside the scope of this book.

By 1900 its name had been abbreviated to the United Billposters' Association and in 1926 it became the British Poster Advertising Association we know today.

In one small respect it differs from most associations. That is its loyalty to its Presidents, or perhaps, it is their loyalty to the Association. The name of Walter Hill, for instance, appears in 1890, 1896, 1902, 1903, 1905, 6, 7 and 8. while G. T. Mills held the post for eight consecutive years.

The London Poster Association was founded in 1890.

The Advertisers

The first of all the Societies to concern itself with advertising in general was the A.P.S., the Advertisers' Protection Society, incorporated as a limited company in 1900.

For nearly ten years a few advertisers had been trying to persuade publishers to disclose their actual sales. The active spirits in the crusade included Fred Oetzman who sold furniture, W. E. Catesby who invented the word 'Lino' and W. B. Warren who sold fountain pens.

By 1900 they had secured enough support to form the Advertisers' Protection Society. Its first Chairman was Deane Bennett, of Trilene, a well-known patent medicine in its time. Its first Secretary was Stanley Baldwin Worth a solicitor and a cousin of Stanley Baldwin, our one time Prime Minister. He was the only paid servant of the Society and his honorarium of £50 a year was eventually increased to £80 a year.

Despite that enormous salary Stanley Worth carried on the job for over twenty years.

In 1904, by which time W. B. Warren of Burge, Warren and Ridgley had taken the chair to hold it, as it turned out, for nearly twenty years, the Society started publishing a confidential *A.P.S. Monthly Circular*.

The *Circular's* purpose was to give members the best available information as to the actual sales of all the important advertising media that the Society could secure.

In May 1908, the *Circular* commenced as a regular feature a 'List of Circulations'. It may be of interest to quote some of the figures it gave.

Daily Express	320,000
Daily Mail	700,000

Daily Mirror	400,000
Daily News	150,000
Daily Telegraph	150,000
The Times	60,000
Manchester Guardian	100,000
Scotsman	80,000
Yorkshire Post	80,000
News of the World	1,250,000
Observer	5,000
People	60,000
Sunday Times	40,000
Punch	80,000

Not unnaturally some of the publishers—all of whom had previously been asked to supply figures—were up in arms when they heard of the figures with which they had been credited.

The *Observer*, then owned by Lord Northcliffe, sued the A.P.S. for libel and the case was heard before Mr. Justice Darling in February 1910.

The charge for libel was ruled out on a technical point and reduced to one of 'publishing a disparaging statement and thereby causing damage'. J. Mortimer Blanch, the famous Advertisement Manager of the *Observer*, proved in the box that the net sales were about 77,000.

Alas for Lord Northcliffe and good fortune for the A.P.S., the *Observer* could not prove any damage and the A.P.S. got judgment and costs.

It was after the *Observer* case that I, in my spare time at the Caxton Publishing Company and taking full advantage of the knowledge of circulations that any mail order advertiser must acquire, took over from Stanley Worth the editorship of the *A.P.S. Circular*.

At least I can claim that I never let them in for a libel action, though my estimate of circulations, particularly in respect of the Provincials, was much lower than that of the first A.P.S. list.

In January 1913, Northcliffe recognised the need for figures and published the complete net sale figures for 1912 of the *Mail*, *Mirror*, *Evening News* and *Weekly Dispatch.* Two days later, the *Chronicle* followed suit and two days later still so did the *Daily News.*

Here was the germ of the Audit Bureau of Circulations aided by a speech at a meeting called by the A.P.S. from Sir George (later Lord) Riddell of the *News of the World.* Riddell urged that such figures should be certified by Chartered Accountants.

Then came the war.

In 1920, the name of the Society was changed to the Incorporated Society of British Advertisers. I.S.B.A.'s own history, ingenuously enough, says this was done 'for no very clear reason'. I could provide plenty! At this time the Society had 200 members and its General Secretary was Alfred H. Angus, later to be joined by Alan Whitworth, who subsequently became its first Director.

Meanwhile, W. B. Warren had resigned his office as Chairman, after nearly thirty years as an inspirer of the movement, and he was succeeded by Thomas Bell, Advertising Manager of Kodak.

And since then I.S.B.A. has gone from strength to strength.

It played the chief part in establishing the Audit Bureau of Circulations in October 1931, and for three years the two organisations ran side by side until in 1934 they separated and Angus became full-time Director of the Bureau while Alan Whitworth succeeded him as General Secretary of I.S.B.A.

The Advertising Agents

The first mention of British Advertising Agents forming an association was in the *Newspaper World* (then called the *Master Printer & Newspaper Owner*) in February 1905, when it published some far from complimentary comments on the new body, although its objects must have seemed admirable.

They were 'to make advertising financially successful and

to prevent advertising of a fraudulent, illegitimate or incompetent character'. They also proposed to restrict membership by imposing tests of 'financial stability and competence'.

Despite this lukewarm welcome, the Advertising Agents Association held its Inaugural Dinner at The Trocadero on 11th May of that year. James Wann was in the Chair and the speakers included S. H. Benson, H. O. Crowther and F. W. Sears.

In the following October, the same paper, then known as the *Newspaper Owner*, chronicled the fact that its incorporation had been granted by the Board of Trade and published a list of the first fifty members of the Incorporated Society of Advertising Agents, fifteen of whom are still members of the Institute of Practitioners in Advertising as it is now known.

One of those who are not was C. A. G. Browne, who achieved unexpected fame and fortune when the Bill for the establishment of Kingsway became Law and it was discovered that his premises in Wych Street had been omitted from the plans and they had to be bought out all on their own.

When, how and why this Society died I have not been able to discover, though I know it was alive in December 1907, because the *Advertising World* of that date carried among whole page advertisements of twenty-seven agents one from the same C. A. G. Browne describing himself as a member.

It is interesting to note that British Advertising Agents got together several years before their American counterparts. The latter started talking about it in 1911 and eventually formed the 'Four A's' in 1917.

The next report of an Advertising Agents' body was in February 1914, when a meeting was held at the old De Keyser's Hotel, on the site of the present Unilever House, attended by representatives of forty agencies. The meeting unanimously decided that it was 'desirable to form an Association of Advertising Agents in the United Kingdom' and appointed a Committee of five to draw up a proposed constitution 'for consideration at a further meeting to be held as soon as possible'.

It would seem that that meeting never came off or, if it did, that it proved abortive because the next news is that during the war, S. H. Benson persuaded some of the bigger agents to meet more or less regularly to hold informal discussions on an agent's problems. The meetings were held in De Keyser's Hotel and were usually presided over by Benson. Among regular attendants were James Wann of T. B. Browne, L. O. Johnson of Mitchell's, H. O. Crowther of Mather and Crowther and one of the directors of Street's.

Eventually these informal meetings resulted in the formation of the Association of British Advertising Agents which a few years later, in 1917, was registered as a company limited by guarantee.

Its first President was L. O. Johnson with his colleague, James Strong, as Chairman. Few of its members remain but E. W. Barney, G. A. Castle, H. G. Saward and C. Harold Vernon are still with us.

Its official organ was *Selling and Advertising*, a monthly magazine which had grown out of the weekly *Printer's Ink*.

I quote now from an article written in 1957 by C. Anstice Brown, Director of the Institute.

'The work of the Association, which was conducted through a Council of fifteen, was in many respects very different from that of the Institute today.

'When the Association was formed, the commission system was by no means established, and was indeed disapproved and challenged by many advertisers and publishers. Many printers and sellers of advertising space and material held themselves out as advertising agents, and dummy agencies existed in considerable numbers. The extent to which rebating was rife may be judged from the remark of the head of a prominent agency who told me that the first question of a prospective client was nearly always, "What are your terms?"

'The situation was not improved by the fact that the Government persistently called for tenders when it wished to issue any advertisements. To combat this state of affairs, the

Association strove with commendable determination to convince advertisers, publishers and the general public that the properly qualified and adequately remunerated advertising agent had a great part to play in the national economy.

'A few years later, in 1922, a step of paramount importance was taken: Lord Northcliffe, after consultation with the Association, issued a form of agreement between agencies and *The Times*, the *Daily Mail* and associated newspapers. Similar agreements were shortly afterwards issued by Hultons, Odhams, and other publishers. These agreements, collectively spoken of as '*The Times* Agreement', were not inaptly referred to by Lord Northcliffe as the "Magna Carta of Publicity".

'The existing agency agreements issued some twenty years later, by the organised bodies of the Press, in which all rebating is prohibited, are merely developments of "*The Times* Agreement".

'While stressing the Association's most important achievement, one must not entirely pass over some of its other accomplishments, such as the founding of the Association of British Advertising Agents Audit Bureau Limited, which was taken over by the Institute and continued to issue booklets of net sales to its members until the present A.B.C. was firmly established.'

I must contradict Anstice Brown in two respects.

(*a*) The commission system *as such* had been established for many years. In 1905 for example there was no important publication which did not allow commission to the little Spottiswoode Advertising Agency. It is true that many other firms, who were not really entitled to it, received commission and that commission splitting was rife, but as a basic principle the commission system was firmly established.

(*b*) Although the Government, through the Stationery Office, had for many years put out the Government advertising for tender, it had broken this rule in 1914.

> None of the probably half-million pounds spent for the Government during the war by the Caxton Advertising Agency had ever been subject to tender so far as the Caxton was concerned.

In 1927 the Association was merged into the present Institute of Practitioners in Advertising. The adoption of the term Practitioner instead of Advertising Agent was due to the fact that there was no means of preventing every little newsagent who accepted 'smalls' for his local paper from calling himself an advertising agent.

Those of us who were original subscribers to the Institute's incorporation know just how valuable its influence has been. Several of us are still alive and kicking. The complete list of subscribers may be of interest. It is as follows:

> P. de G. Benson, E. M. I. Buxton, W. H. Carr, G. A. Castle, J. Coote, Eric Field, E. H. Godbold, A. J. Greenly, Leslie Harwood, L. Jackson, L. O. Johnson, H. L. Mather, H. G. Saward, James Strong, R. J. Sykes, R. Winter Thomas, C. Harold Vernon.

The first President of the Institute was Philip de G. Benson, son of the founder of S. H. Benson Ltd. (S. H. B. having died in July 1914). Lionel Jackson was the Hon. Treasurer and Ralph Winter Thomas, the Hon. Secretary.

The witness to all the signatures was C. Anstice Brown.

For several years the Institute adhered rigidly to the original idea of confining its membership to British Advertising Agents and excluding any subsidiaries of American concerns.

It was because I got tired of being in a minority of one on a point I regarded as of vital importance that I resigned from the Council.

Now and for years we have welcomed them and have grown in stature and in influence thereby.

Next the Consultants

I am not sure that next is the appropriate word.

The Agents may have tried to get together and actually formed Associations before the Consultants but the Consultants set up their present constitution before the Agents settled down to their present, permanent form, by founding the Incorporated Society of Advertisement Consultants in 1910.

The doyen of the profession was undoubtedly the Thomas Russell, to whom I owe so much.

When I took over the Editorship of *Printers' Ink*, the Consultants had no association but they were very valuable to me. They were the only people from whom I could secure intelligent and unbiased articles on advertising without having to pay for them.

It was a pity that whenever I published such a contribution S. H. Benson, who had a supervisory function to perform, charged me with publishing something 'inimical to the agency system'.

S. H. B. was obviously obsessed with a quite unfounded fear of Consultants as a whole.

Reverting to the Consultants, the Incorporated Society of Advertisement Consultants was founded on 10 April 1910, with a range of objects which included 'To support and protect the character, status and interest of the profession of Advertisement Consultant and to promote honourable practice', and amongst other things 'to conduct examinations in advertising'. The Founder Members were Thomas Russell, Geo. V. Briscoe, Robert Donald, Cyril Mortimer, Marcus Heber Smith, Hopton Hadley and F. J. Hortop.

The original intention was to limit membership to men or women—not being advertising agents—earning their remuneration by fees alone and not by commissions from newspapers.

In 1932 the basis of membership was broadened to include men or women holding responsible executive positions in important advertising firms, it being held that their duties to large concerns was in fact in the nature of consultancy work. Amongst those who took an active part in the Society in that way were the following: Commander H. J. H. Ellis (I.C.I.), Bertram E. Kent (Allen & Hanbury's), W. Buchanan Taylor (J. Lyons & Co.), Clifford J. Harrison (Horlicks), Charles J. Rose (Scott & Bowne Ltd.), Geo. Warden (Cunard White Star Co.), Gordon Hargreave (Independent Consultant), John Kirkwood (Independent Consultant).

The Society conducted the first public Examinations in Advertising in 1925, with an examining Board comprised of Thomas Russell, P. Garfield Blake, William T. Day, Henry S. H. Ellis, Hopton Hadley, John Kirkwood, Herbert S. Peacocke, Dudley W. Walton and William T. Moss.

The Society held its last Final Examination in 1931, the Advertising Association by that time having established its own examinations, which have had such a tremendous influence.

The Advertising Managers

Like the Agents, the Advertising Managers had an abortive start. Their first effort was the Advertising Managers' Club.

According to Clifford Martin, one of the few, if not the only, surviving founder members, the Club was founded about 1907. Its other original members included Cecil Maryon of Columbia Gramophones, Noel Godber at that time of St. Ivel Cheese and later of Boots, Ronnie Gaze of Harrods, Freddie Le Queux of Whiteley's, L. Hartland Swann of Icilma, S. P. Hunt of Catesby's, Rudolph Hagen of Cadbury's, Oswald Strickland and J. Huband.

When it died I have not been able to discover but the *World's Press News* of 22 September 1932, published a letter from Hunt urging that it should be revived. Whence originated our present, flourishing Advertising Managers' Association.

The Advertising Association

As mentioned in a previous chapter, the first attempt to form an association which would include Advertisers, Publishers, Billposters, Advertising Agents and all concerned with advertising was made by the Thirty Club before the first World War under the title of the British Association of Advertising.

It was formally founded at a meeting at the Hotel Cecil in June 1914. Sir William Lever (later Lord Leverhulme) was elected President, John Hart was the Hon. Secretary and P. C. Burton, the Hon. Treasurer. Its first action was to send a delegation of twenty members to the Convention of the Associated Advertising Clubs of America at Toronto. Of them at least four made speeches at the Convention: J. J. O'Neill, Wareham Smith, Percy Burton and C. F. Higham.

The first World War put an untimely end to the B.A.A. and it was not till February 1926, that the ideal was realised in the Advertising Association as we know it today. Andrew Milne was the first Hon. Secretary and Arthur Chadwick, its Hon. Treasurer.

It would be tempting to tell the full story of the A.A. and the part it played and is still playing in the development of the industry, but that story does not really fall within the scope of this book and is best left to others.

8. Advertising's Own Press

THIS LITTLE book would obviously be incomplete without some reference to the early days of advertising's own trade journals.

America had one as early as 1888 but it was not till ten years later that a young would-be engineer of Birstall in Yorkshire, called Charles Baker, changed his mind and published the first independent journal dealing with advertising and every other aspect of the newspaper business.

On 5 January 1898 appeared the first issue of a twenty-four-page demy-quarto *Newspaper Owner and Manager*. It is worth quoting from its first 'Leader':

'There is, so far as we are aware, no journal in this country that is devoted to the interests of newspaper production. The agents who sell the newspapers have their own organs, but the thousands of business firms by whom such papers are produced have absolutely no trade journal in which to voice their views, record their developments, or cater in any way for their information and benefit.

'One gathering ground for our news will be the newspaper Press itself. If a paper comes out in an enlarged form, or printed for the first time from the reel, or set by machine, we shall have a few lines recording the fact. If a paper makes some striking departure or takes a lead in any direction, we shall tell our readers all about it.

'We shall not stop here. We shall tell of new ads. that are being issued and give warnings of those to be avoided. We shall advocate needed libel, postal, and other reforms, publish practical articles on mechanical, publishing, and counting-house methods, collect views and opinions on the Press questions of the day from those best qualified to deal with them, and generally endeavour to adapt our pages to the taste and requirements of the somewhat critical body of readers to whom we shall appeal.'

(With minor modifications, much of this might apply today.)

One of the points that were strongly advocated in early issues of the *Newspaper Owner and Manager* was the more frequent use of the half-tone block in newspapers. In 1898 the half-tone illustration was a rarity in newspapers, and it was really not until the twentieth century had begun that there was any great activity in that direction.

In this field of extension of newspaper illustration, Charles Baker was certainly one of the pioneers, for in the 'nineties he was syndicating portrait blocks and biographies to provincial papers.

It was to produce the paper that Baker became one of the earliest users of the Linotype in this country. The first handbook on its use was actually published by the *Newspaper Owner*.

In its long life, the paper's name was changed from time to time but eventually settled down to the *Newspaper World*.

For a long time, however, the paper paid little attention to advertising. Indeed it was not till the spring of 1910 that it devoted a regular whole page to the subject under the heading 'Things that Matter in Advertising' and over the signature 'George Warrington', a *nom de plume* of George Edgar, once Editor of the *Advertising World* and a contributor of mine on *Printers' Ink*. Even this page was directed more to the publisher than to the advertiser.

By the end of 1913, the paper had adopted its final title but it had given up its weekly page on advertising and it never received much advertising support from publishers or advertising agents. It did, however, announce in 1914 that, apart from its wide subscription list, its sales in Fleet Street alone were over 1,700 copies a week.

The *Newspaper World* survived both World Wars and died a lamented death in 1953.

The first independent journal purely concerned with advertising made its appearance in December 1901.

That was the *Advertising World*. Its first issue consisted of thirty-two quarto pages, containing thirty-five advertisements of various sizes.

Twenty-five were from publishers, six from advertising agents, two from engravers and two 'miscellaneous'.

Six years later its December issue, printed throughout in two colours, consisted of 160 large octavo pages and carried 137 advertisements, classified as follows:

Publishers	67
Advertising Agents	26
Engravers	7
Billposters	10
Printers	10
Miscellaneous	17

Of the advertising agents only nine are still alive: Dixon's West End, Erwoods', Haddon's, Keymer's, Mather & Crowther, Mitchell's, Sell's, Smith's and Street's.

Of the sixty-seven publications only twenty survive.

The *Advertising World* was one of, if not the first, publishing efforts of the Berry brothers who later became famous as Lord Camrose and Lord Kemsley. W. E. ('Bill') Berry (Lord Camrose), who was born in Merthyr Tydfil in 1879 and had his first newspaper experience on the *Merthyr Times*, came to London in 1893 and joined the editorial staff of the *Investors' Guardian*. In December 1901, practically without influence or capital, he started the *Advertising World*. A month or two later he was joined by his younger brother Gomer Berry (Lord Kemsley) and it was not till the autumn of 1909 that they sold the magazine to J. C. Akerman, J. R. Charter, who had relieved Bill Berry of the Editorship in 1905, remaining in that position.

As an indication of what the *Advertising World* had come to mean by then I should mention that on 17 December 1909 at the Hotel Cecil a dinner was given in the Berry brothers' honour attended by over one hundred of the people who at that time mattered in advertising. Sir George Riddell was in the chair and the speakers included Ralston Balch, James Wann, Wareham Smith and J. Murray Allison. Almost the only survivor of the dinner is our present Lord Kemsley.

A beautiful specimen of typography was produced in calf binding with a print order of five copies. Lord Kemsley has lent me a copy and it would give a great thrill to the descendants of the speakers, all of whom have whole page illustrations, to see how handsome their grandparents were.

After about two years Akerman sold the magazine to Coleman who had been head of the *Times of India.* From his hands it passed into those of Industrial Newspapers Ltd. and in 1932-3 Industrial Newspapers disposed of it to Capt. Crewdson. Finally, the latter, three or four years later, sold it to Tibor Korda who merged it into the *World's Press News.*

Crewdson and Korda were both victims of the 'Blitz', the former while fire-watching, the latter by falling masonry outside the R.A.C. in Pall Mall.

In the early 1900's there was also a monthly *Advertising* issued by Smith's of 100 Fleet Street. Even Smith's do not know when it started or when and why it died.

Meanwhile, S. H. Benson, who had for years published a very useful biennial handbook, selling at ten and six, called *Benson's Facts*, had been casting envious eyes on the famous American weekly advertising journal *Printers' Ink*, and in 1909 he made arrangements with its U.S. publishers to bring out an English edition of the paper.

The original *Printers' Ink* was established by an American Advertising Agent, called George P. Rowell, in July 1888 and was the first regular advertising journal in the world. It was also the first 'pocket size' publication in the world. The reason for this format was simple. Rowell had a printing plant which could not cope with a bigger size.

At first started as a monthly, *Printers' Ink* was converted into a weekly two years later but retained its 'pocket' size until January 1942.

Naturally enough, the English *Printer's Ink* followed the format of its American parent and for the first year any articles reprinted from the American edition carried a baby 'Stars and Stripes' alongside the heading.

Benson employed Thomas Russell, the first of all British Advertising Consultants, to act as Editor and the little paper was reasonably successful, sufficiently so at any rate for Benson in a year or two to form a separate company, called Printers' Ink Ltd.

Its Managing Director and Managing Editor was Jesse D. Hampton, who had just given up the same position on the American *Printers' Ink*. The other Directors included Benson, H. O. Crowther of Mather & Crowther, James Wann of T. B. Browne and James Strong of Mitchell's. I was assistant Editor and Secretary of the company.

In June 1910 Jesse Hampton decided there was no great future in a paper which found it difficult to sell its space at £3 a page and retired to more exciting prospects in Hollywood.

I succeeded him as Editor and in my turn was succeeded by T. Swinborne Sheldrake who had been Editor of *The Times Trade Supplement*.

Sheldrake knew all about high commerce but he lacked the one essential quality of the editor of an advertising journal. He had no faith in advertising!

Soon after he took over, it ceased to be a weekly, changed its format and became a full sized monthly 'glossy' under the name of *Selling and Advertising*.

When the war came, it died an inglorious death.

Almost simultaneously with the conversion of *Printers' Ink* into a monthly, Jack Akerman started the *Advertiser's Weekly*. I well remember in late 1912 spending a week-end at Jack's charming little house at Esher and helping him with the layout of his first dummy. Count it to our prescience that, although it has many more pages now, the *Advertiser's Weekly*'s format is basically the same today.

The first issue appeared on 19 April 1913 under the editorship of the George Warrington who as mentioned above had been contributing to the *Newspaper Owner*.

Printers' Ink's sales as a weekly had never topped the 3,000 mark and it took the *Advertiser's Weekly* quite some time to approach that figure. Indeed, when T. J. Zimmerman acquired it in 1919, it consisted of eight pages and its circulation had dwindled to 'a few hundreds'.

Now its sales are over 10,000 and A.B.C. figures at that!

Zimmerman had begun his publishing career in this country with a monthly called *System* and under his able guidance the *Weekly* took on a new lease of life. At the time of his death in 1952, at the age of seventy-two, its eight pages had grown to over fifty.

In its long history, despite Zeppelin bombs, blitzes and only too accurately guided missiles, it has never missed an issue.

Its Twenty-first Anniversary number issued in April 1934 ran to 140 pages, most of them in colour. It included testimonies from Lord Riddell, Lord Astor, Lord Beaverbrook, Lord Rothermere, Lord Camrose, Lord Ebbisham, Lord Luke, Lord Marshall, Sir Herbert Austin and the heads of almost every agency in the country.

In closing this chapter I cannot do better than repeat the words of my then boss, Vernon J. Reveley, about the *Advertiser's Weekly*. 'Hoping it will be as successful in the future as it has been in the past.'

9. Just what is Advertising?

(This chapter may seem out of place in this book. It is not in any material way historic and it does not come within my self-imposed chronological orbit. What it does do is to present the sincere convictions of one who has been in advertising for over fifty years. E. F.)

IN ALL the years I have spent in the business I have never found a satisfactory definition of advertising. The dictionaries are useless. The best the Oxford Concise, for instance, can provide is 'Notify, warn, inform, make generally known'.

Advertising is vastly more than that. Advertising is one of the prime factors in the steady growth of the world's standard of living. Without advertising, without the demand it could be depended upon to create, no manufacturer could have afforded to lay down the plant necessary for the mass production, which alone has brought the luxuries of modern life within the reach of all.

Nor, indeed, without advertising and what it could do would any manufacturer have been interested in improving old lines or developing new ones.

As this chapter was being written, Lord Heyworth, head of the great Unilever concern, pointed out to his shareholders that, but for advertising, housewives would still be buying soap by the yard. He also pointed out that in almost every country every one of Unilever's products had increased in price by a much lower percentage than the general Cost of Living Index of the country concerned. But for the £83,000,000 spent throughout the world by Unilever in the past year, that state of affairs would have been impossible.

Yet in his intensely valuable speech he did not refer to one vital fact.

Advertising is not simply a means of selling. It can be, and usually is, part of the product. With medicinal lines this is indisputable. It can and must inspire the faith which would otherwise be given by the doctor's 'bedside manner'.

Women—and men—buy Aspro and get relief from it which they would not get from a tablet just labelled Acetyl-salicylic Acid. They might get the same relief if Acetyl-salicylic were advertised as well as Aspro, but it is not.

The result is that Aspro plays a bigger part in relieving human suffering just *because* it is advertised.

The same thing applies in varying degrees to all sorts of goods. If a woman buys a detergent believing that it 'washes whiter', it *will* wash whiter, possibly because she uses it with greater confidence and follows the instructions more closely. If a man buys a motor car, partly because it gives 'more miles per gallon', he will drive it in such a way that he *does* get more miles per gallon.

One could go on giving countless illustrations of this, probably the most fundamental function which advertising can serve.

But for this often ignored fact, advertising could not bring the marketing successes that it does.

In my own limited experience I know something of what the right sort of advertising can do.

In a previous chapter I referred to the fact that at times in the first World War Press advertising and nothing but advertising, without any speeches or special recruiting 'drives', persuaded men to volunteer and risk their lives, when up to the day they read the advertisements, they had refrained from doing so. Could one seek a more outstanding example of what advertising can do?

Is it, then, surprising that I can quote from my own experience examples like the four that follow. I have chosen them from the medicinal field, firstly, because that particular market is one where results are more easily traceable than in other markets, and, secondly, because merchandising and salesmanship play a smaller part in that trade than they do in many others.

My first example is Maclean's Stomach Powder.

Maclean's Stomach Powder's existence today is entirely due to an initial expenditure of no less a sum than £36.

The line had been on the market for some time without moving off the shelves and in 1931, before abandoning the line, the makers decided to try one small advertising experiment in Preston. The only 'merchandising' was that the local salesman was instructed to persuade half the retail chemists in Preston to take in a token stock of not more than half a dozen bottles, if necessary on sale or return. The reason for the small size of this quota was to ensure that any sales would be reflected as rapidly as possible.

When that degree of distribution had been secured, two 3-inch single column advertisements were inserted in the *Lancashire Daily Post* each week for six weeks at a total cost of £36. In that period that small expenditure showed a *nett* profit of over £100.

The same policy of securing 50 per cent. distribution before releasing advertising was followed step by step throughout the country with the result that inside three years sales were running at about £30,000 a month.

An example of how the right sort of advertising can revive an old established line is provided by the case of Wincarnis.

In the early 1920's, Coleman & Co. Ltd. ran for a year or so a series of beautiful advertisements with illustrations by artists of the calibre of Bernard Partridge. They were outstanding as advertisements but they were over the heads of potential buyers and the result was that one day the half-yearly balance sheet showed a loss running well into five figures.

Coleman's decided to spend 20 per cent. less for the next six months on entirely different copy and hoped to increase sales by 25 per cent. in order to break even at the end of the year. In the crucial six months their sales increased by 55 per cent. and they finished with a nett profit equal to what their loss had been at the half-year.

There had been no change in their merchandising except to cut out a Bonus Scheme and the weather was normal.

The improvement was entirely due to the advertising.

At the beginning of the second World War a pharmaceutical manufacturer bought a laxative salt called Juno-Junipah, which had been marketed and advertised for two years with so little success that its sales had dropped to less than £5 per month. An experiment with new copy on a tiny scale produced immediate results and within a few years the line had become the second or third seller in its highly competitive market. His 'selling' organisation never consisted of more than three 'part-time' salesmen and practically nothing was done in the way of Direct Mail.

His success was entirely due to advertising.

To quote a very recent case. The famous Lloyd's Adrenaline Cream was launched with an initial expenditure of £68 on an 8-inch double column in the *Yorkshire Evening Post* and the *Yorkshire Evening News*. The only 'merchandising' was to get five chemists in Leeds to lay in stocks on the promise that their names would be mentioned in the advertisements. None of the other chemists in the West Riding were even informed of the line's existence. The response was startling. One chain chemist in Wakefield, the morning after the *Yorkshire Evening News* advertisement appeared, telegraphed an order for five gross five-shilling size and two and a half gross seven-and-six size. In less than a fortnight over £1,000 worth of orders had been received.

Now, of course, Lloyd's Adrenaline Cream is by far the paramount Rheumatic Remedy.

I do not suggest for a moment that, even with proper marketing support, advertising is always successful and I am not ignoring the importance of intrinsic merit in the product, but the mere fact that it can at times produce results like these with so little support is of vital interest.

I am sure that every advertising agent could cite similar and even more striking examples of just what advertising can do.

The very power, however, of advertising and its importance to the National Economy create an urgent need for a practical definition of 'advertising'.

Despite all that advertising men and women have done to help manufacturers and industrialists and thereby played a not inconsiderable part in the raising of the Nation's standard of living, they have done very little to make the public realise just what they have done and are doing.

The consequence is that, although most people would agree that advertising in general was a good thing, when it comes to the particular things they buy themselves, the great majority believe in their heart of hearts that the goods could be cheaper, if the makers did not spend so much on advertising.

Commercial Television has aggravated this feeling very seriously. There are few regular viewers who do not believe, quite sincerely, that if Omo did not say so often every night that it 'washes brighter', it could reduce its price in the shop.

This public belief is a grave and growing menace to advertising and in the ultimate end to our National Economy.

It should not be beyond the ability of the advertising profession to educate the mass public to the real situation, but to do so it must be factual and, above all, truthful.

Lord Heyworth set an excellent example, but if others are to follow suit, they should know what is an 'advertising expense'.

In the old days this was easy. It was what one spent on advertising, in the Press or on posters. Direct Mail was practically unknown. Showcards were negligible. Display containers did not exist.

Now advertising, or at least the work carried out by an

Advertising Agent, has spread so widely and become so complicated, that there is grave danger that a quite unbiased statistician, seeking to compare advertising costs with sales figures, would include among advertising costs a great many things which are not advertising at all.

Take Market Research for instance. It is quite sensible for a manufacturer, contemplating a new line, to ask his Advertising Agent to put his Research Department to work ascertaining the potential demand.

But what on earth has it to do with advertising as a selling expense? The manufacturer would have had to find out the situation even if he never intended to advertise at all.

The same thing applies to investigation into distribution.

Information as to the strength and locality of distribution can help in planning the allocation of advertising and improve the results it brings, but it is not an advertising expense in itself.

Showcards and counter cards or display containers are, one must assume, advertising, but what percentage of the cost of an ornamental carton should be regarded as advertising?

If so, what about the cut glass bottle of an expensive perfume?

Again, are the temporary price cuts, so popular in some trades, advertising? Lord Heyworth in his speech treats them as if they were, but is not that stretching the word unfairly? They often are the subject of advertising. They may in the end reduce the amount available for advertising. But neither fact makes them in themselves advertising.

If a temporary price reduction is advertising, what is a permanent one?

The whole problem is, I know, very complicated, but if our statistics are to be of any real value in educating the public and the politicians they should be on a common basis.

And such a definition should not be beyond the wits of the great interests concerned.

Any propaganda certainly should not take the form of a

comparison of the total amount spent on advertising throughout the country with the total National Income. Such a comparison is completely unrealistic and, if used for this purpose, savours of rank dishonesty.

And in such a grave issue truth, if wisely propagated, will prevail.

10. A Postscript and an Apology

I SUPPOSE it is natural to look back on the past with regrets which may in fact be completely illusory.

All the same it does seem to me that in the old days there was a feeling of adventure and excitement and personal interest which we do not enjoy nowadays.

Probably it is largely due to the growth of our 'population'. Half a century ago, we advertising people formed a small community, competing hotly with each other, but knowing our competitors personally or at least knowing of them.

In such a small community those with outstanding character were real personalities.

Another factor in this feeling of adventure was that the power of advertising was only just being realised. Gone were the days when the best an advertiser, who wanted to use the *Telegraph*, could do was to take a whole single column and divide it into twenty-four single column inches, each repeating the same half-dozen words, perhaps blessed with 'Drop Caps'. Now advertisements were beginning to be advertisements and producing real and tangible results.

There was a new and intensely satisfying feeling of achievement.

Finally, I feel sorry for the lads in a modern agency.

In the days of which I am writing, blockmakers and typesetters worked regular night shifts, at times all through the week-end.

It was no uncommon thing for me to be sent with a sketch

to the blockmakers in the evening, to wait while the block was being made—often to watch it being done—and then to take it to the typesetters to be inserted in the forme, so that complete, corrected proofs could be in the office first thing next day.

And Allison could proudly show it to his latest prospect in the morning.

We boys found it fun and were only too happy to do it without any thought of asking for 'overtime'.

May I be allowed to say that I have enjoyed almost every day I have spent in the advertising business, and that, if I had my choice over again, I would not have had it altered.

If this story has seemed at times to be limping, halting and disjointed, that was an inevitable consequence of its object, which was to provide an accurate, historical record of the advance of advertising in the first quarter of the twentieth century.

The search for accuracy and its occasional discovery rendered any smooth and elegant flow of language impossible. Almost every chapter has had to be re-written or at least altered heavily, because just as it was about to be closed down, some fact discovered in one chapter called for modification in another.

Forgive its manifold faults, and occasional inaccuracies. It is as accurate as I have been able to make it.

In the course of that endeavour I have shown chapters to friends who might be able to help me.

What has struck me more than anything is the interest they have shown when they suddenly met the name of a man they had known years ago and completely forgotten.

So it seems that it might be worthwhile mentioning some of the many who have helped me on my not very glorious way.

I must confine myself to those who have passed over, because I must leave my few remaining contemporaries to tell their own stories.

Nor should I include in this chapter a duplication of what has already been written in previous ones.

I give these little reminiscences in alphabetical order because there is no other appropriate order. There must be many other friends I should have mentioned but I hope their shades will forgive me.

Akerman, John Camille

Known to all Fleet Street as 'Jack', Akerman came into my orbit very early. After spending some time in the Merchant Navy, he had become one of a group of ambitious young advertising men, including the Berry brothers, Ashby Goodall, J. Murray Allison, Bill Wallace and Archie Martin, H. E. Morgan, Macleod Moore and other kindred spirits. Just what he was doing then I do not remember. Indeed my first real acquaintance with him began in 1909 when he took over the *Advertising World*. After disposing of that magazine, he started the *Advertiser's Weekly*. In 1915 he became Advertisement Manager of *The Times*, which post he gave up during the war to join the Deputy Controller of Auxiliary Shipbuilding as a Major in the Royal Engineers. After the war he started *Nash's Weekly* and when that paper ceased publication he, much to his own profit, became head of the *Daily Chronicle*.

Allison, J. Murray

Jim was the second advertising man I ever met. A fellow Australian, he was then in 1905 in his first job as a canvasser at £3 a week plus commission for a small advertising agency. (Spottiswoode's.) As a salesman he was unequalled. I saw him grow in stature and in income till he became the Advertisement Manager who put *The Times* on the advertising 'map'. Till Allison took over the job, *The Times* was hardly considered a medium to use except for financial, property and similar advertising. Allison changed all that. He conceived and produced supplements of all sorts. If they involved foreign countries, he went himself to Russia, South

America, South Africa—anywhere where sufficient business could be secured.

Whether he got on with Northcliffe or not I do not know but I think he left Printing House Square because he wanted to be a publisher himself. As such, he was not very successful, but when he died a great many of us felt we had lost a very, very good friend.

Incidentally, as a poet some of his verse was delightful.

Barnes, Horace

Once an important copywriter with Derricks', he was one of the Americans who enlisted in the British Army in the early days of the first World War. On demobilisation he went on the 'Halls' with what became a very successful 'act'. He would ask someone in the audience to name a subject and someone else to suggest a tune. Horace would, impromptu, sing words that made sense and rhymed, if they did not always scan, in a very colourable imitation of the tune. It was in a way an advanced calypso and brought him a much higher income than he had ever made in advertising, let alone as a private in the Fusiliers.

Beable, William Henry

Father of our present 'Joe', W. H. Beable spent his early years in the States, finally becoming publisher of the *Anglo-American Times* in Trenton, New Jersey. Returning to England during the Boer War, he joined S. H. Benson Ltd. as Chief Copywriter and subsequently became the first employee to join the Board.

Later he became Sales and Advertising Manager of 'Vi-Cocoa'.

At the outbreak of the first World War he joined Martins Ltd. and organised a 'Tobacco Fund for the Troops' on behalf of some 120 Provincial Newspapers.

In 1915 he led his own Trade Delegation to Russia and on his return became Sales and Advertising Manager for Carreras.

Retiring through ill-health, he built up a Mail Order business supplying speeches for ambitious orators, including Bishops, M.Ps., Mayors and leaders of Industry.

Benson, Philip de G.

Succeeding his father as head of Benson's, Philip carried on where his father left off, not only in the development of the business itself but in matters such as the organisation of the agencies. He was the first President of the I.P.A. As mentioned in an early chapter, Philip's invitation to a fellow Dulwich boy to join Benson's was probably a turning point in my life.

Blanch, J. Mortimer

Mortimer Blanch was one of the outstanding Advertisement Managers of the 1900's. He started in business as a bank clerk and at the head office of the Westminster one day assisted in taking down the clock for cleaning. It was collected by two men and a cart and has never been seen again. Bank raids in those days were evidently modest things, though apparently pretty brazen.

Leaving banking, Blanch secured a job with the *Schoolmaster*, the leading scholastic paper of the time. Then he joined first the *Gentlewoman* and later *Black & White* as Advertisement Manager. In 1904 or 1905 Northcliffe asked him to become Advertisement Manager of the *Observer* and despite changes of ownership he held that position till he retired in 1930.

When Northcliffe sold the *Observer* to Lord Astor—a deal negotiated by Blanch and J. L. Garvin, then its Editor—Blanch became Advertisement Manager of the *Pall Mall Gazette* as well.

At the time Blanch joined the *Observer*, its print order, I am told by Tom Blanch, was about 2,000 and its advertising revenue about £90 a week.

Mortimer Blanch was, of course, the father of Eric, Tom and Jack Blanch.

Buchanan, Taylor W.

Known to everybody as 'Bucky' he had about as wide an acquaintance as anyone I ever met. An apt raconteur, it was difficult to mention a name without him having a good story to tell. In his book, *Shake the Bottle*, his index runs to six columns covering journalism, the theatre, the prize ring, business big and little, Hollywood, bootlegging, the Irish troubles—there is hardly a sphere of activity on which he does not touch.

Bucky started his career as an editorial messenger on the *Manchester Guardian*. Thence he went to Hulton's where he spent fourteen years in all sorts of editorial positions.

In advertising he made his name as the Advertising Manager of Lyons who was responsible for the one time popular slogan: 'Where's George? He's gone to Lyonch!' He was also the creator of 'Nippy' in which connection he persuaded Anna Neagle, then a chorus girl, to pose as the original waitress. 'Bucky' retired through ill-health in 1953, having been a member of I.S.A.C. since 1932.

Burton, Percy C.

Brother-in-law of Northcliffe and father of the Basil Burton who runs the *World's Press News* and allied journals. Our first meeting was somewhat unconventional. I caught him literally 'with his pants down'. He was then head of P. C. Burton & Co. in Essex Street, Strand, and I was sent to persuade him to take shares in Printer's Ink Ltd. Although he was changing to play golf, he saw me and, perhaps because of his predicament, I left with an application for twenty-five shares of £1 each. I was to come across him many times afterwards in business and in the Army and always to my benefit. A charming personality, Percy was very good looking, popular everywhere and a good soldier who had fought in the South African War. In the first World War he rose to be a full Colonel at G.H.Q.

Bussy, Fred E.

At one time Advertisement Manager of the *Evening News*, Fred Bussy found his greatest fame as organiser of the Ideal Homes Exhibition, a task he handled so well that the Exhibition's success exceeded all anticipations and now grows in importance and profit every year.

As a slight indication of Carmelite House's early failure to foresee its potentialities, the title *Ideal Home* was allowed to be registered by Odham's for its well-known magazine.

Bussy, Herbert M.

As tall as and as obviously a brother of 'Fred'—Bert Bussy joined the *Daily Mail* in 1906 and worked with Fred in the paper's special publicity department until four years later he became Assistant Advertisement Manager of the *Evening News*. In 1914 he was appointed Advertisement Manager of the *News of the World*, where he remained until he retired for reasons of health in June 1938. He was an original member of the Advertising Committee of the N.P.A. for many years.

Campbell, Brigadier-General Neville

I first met the retired Indian Army Major, when way back in 1910 we were both working for Benson's. When I found myself more or less running *Printer's Ink*, I brought Campbell in as Advertisement Manager at £3 a week and *no* commission. He left that job about the same time as I did, joining J. Bewsher at the *Sphere*. When the first World War broke out he became Adjutant-General in Mesopotamia.

After the war, when Harrison formed Illustrated Newspapers, Campbell became Advertisement Director, a post he held till he died. There he was famous for the 'Beauty Chorus' he gathered round him to secure orders for the papers under his control and, posthumously, for the fact that he owed a lot more to the Tax Authorities than the Estate could pay.

Carter, George

I first worked with George Carter when he was Managing Director of the London branch of the famous Berlin Advertising Agents, Rudolf Mosse, handling German business in the U.K. and British business on the Continent. Erwoods' had worked with Rudolf Mosse for years. Rudolph Mosse's German business included, I believe, Odol Mouthwash—bought after the first World War by Coleman's of Norwich—and a heavily advertised slimming device called the Punkt Roller.

George died tragically by accidentally electrocuting himself in his bath.

Chadwick, Arthur

Arthur Chadwick was probably the man who really introduced 'Direct Mail' advertising to England. At least he was the first to provide advertisers and agents with the addressing service we now take as a matter of course. His 'Reliable Addressing Co.' could provide the lists of addresses and carry out the whole job. Where he got his addresses from I do not know but he started before Kelly's established their copyright. Later on the firm blossomed out as an agency under the name of Amalgamated Publicity Services. He was one of the delegates to Philadelphia.

Cheshire, John

John Cheshire lives in my memory as a charming and to me at that time elderly gentleman who headed the delegation to America in 1923. Though he was Advertising Manager of Lever Brothers he had not been particularly prominent in advertising circles and I imagine that his choice for that position was partly, of course, because he was President of the Thirty Club, but almost as much because he was too nice for his selection to give rise to any jealousies. In America he was an outstanding success as the embodiment of the perfect English gentleman.

Clark, Samson

Everybody called him 'Sammy', if not always to his face, because like all little men he had a high sense of dignity and importance. Despite which, he could not make a speech—and he made many—without prefacing it by saying, 'I know that what I am going to say is of no importance, but . . .'

Founder of the flourishing Advertising Agency which still bears his name, Sammy was quite a character and played an important part in the growth of modern advertising, particularly in work for the big Department Stores.

Sammy made surprising news in December 1913 when for some reason or another he was assaulted by footpads on his way home to his charming house at East Molesey.

He died an unexpected and greatly regretted death in Central Africa.

Coram, Sydney G.

In 1905 Sydney Coram was Advertisement Manager of the *Westminster Gazette*, one of London's several evening papers distinguished among other things by the fact that it was printed on green paper. By 1907 he had joined Pearson's. Tall and distinguished looking, he was a prominent member of the Fleet Street Club.

Crawford, Sir William

One of the many 'Scots' who have crossed the Border to seek fame and fortune in London and one who succeeded above the average. His first London job was, I believe, with Potter's but I got to know Bill well when he joined Charles Bridges in forming a small agency, called Bridges and Crawford Ltd., somewhere in Kingsway. In perhaps a couple of years, Bridges retired and the firm became W. S. Crawford Ltd.

Everyone knows how the firm has grown and how he

received a Knighthood for his work in connection with the Empire Marketing Board. Bill played a big part in the organisation of advertising and his old friends will remember the fervour with which he waved the 'Fierry Torrch'.

Emanuel, Philip

A fellow Australian, Philip Emanuel came to England in 1895 and at fifteen became secretary to a South African millionaire at thirty-five shillings a week. He was so keen on advertising that when Alfred Johnson offered him a job as a clerk at Newnes at twenty shillings he jumped at it. At that time he had to walk five miles to work from the East End and five miles home—except on pay day.

Eventually Johnson put him on to selling space on back covers of sixpenny novels and he did it well enough to be sent to Manchester to make a go of Newnes' very unprofitable branch there.

Philip succeeded sufficiently to keep the job for nine years.

In January 1914 on a visit to London John Hart introduced him to J. S. Elias (later Lord Southwood), Manager of Odham's, then a purely printing firm. Elias persuaded Philip to join him and between them they created the Odham's we know today.

Philip was a President of the Thirty Club and helped to found the Regent. He was a member of the Council of N.A.B.S. for twenty-five years until his death in 1955.

Feilden, Theodore J. V.

Theo Feilden, who died three years ago at the ripe age of ninety-two, had a quite unique career. A personal friend of George VI he received on his ninetieth birthday the congratulations of H.M. the Queen and the Queen Mother. In 1887, he founded what subsequently became the *Engineering Review*. In 1908 he joined *The Times* as Advertisement Manager of its *Engineering Supplement* and in 1916 he acted in the same capacity for the *Trade Supplement*. Theo left *The Times* in 1917 and founded the *Empire Mail*.

Feilden served in the Boer War and in 1914 he helped to organise the fleet of taxis which saved Paris.

At the end of the second World War, at the age of eighty-one, he went to Germany as an Honorary Colonel to report on post-war conditions.

Godley, Gilbert A.

'Gil', as his golfing friends will recall, was a tall, very heavily built man with tiny feet. It must have been torture to him to finish even one round, let alone the two ordained for most meetings. Wareham Smith's book mentions him as one of the first canvassers on the *Mail* but most of us remember him as the genial and very successful Advertisement Manager of the *Daily Mirror*.

Godley had the moral courage, when he had achieved success, of buying a property in the snobbish village of Balcombe in Sussex, where his father had been a jobbing gardener and where he himself became a prominent member of the local Council.

Goodall, Toby

Younger brother of the Ashby Goodall to whom I owe my presence in such an exciting business as advertising, I found Toby ensconced as what we then called Publicity Manager of *The Times* in 1919, when I became Advertisement Manager of that august journal. Toby later became Advertising Manager of White Horse Whisky. When Prohibition was obviously going to be repealed, Toby was instructed to go to the States and lay plans for handling the 'new' market. He came to me for advice and introductions. Whether he used either I do not know but he returned covered with glory and triumphantly successful.

Hadley, Hopton

What do I remember of him? As a person very little, but as one of the first consultants quite a lot. As a matter of fact, he was more a free-lance copywriter than anything. At that he was a great success. As a mail order copywriter he was unexcelled and he had the financial acumen to charge, not a fee for his actual copy, but a percentage of the money spent on space.

Hadley was one of the founders and for many years Vice-President of the Incorporated Society of Advertisement Consultants.

Hart, John

John was a very likeable and very able chap but somewhat of a rolling stone. I first got to know him as Advertisement Manager of *London Opinion*. Before then he had spent several years in Paris in some capacity connected with advertising and not unnaturally was a fluent French speaker. He left *London Opinion* to form a not very successful advertising agency called Hart & Harford. He also ran the John Hassall School of Drawing, Hassall being the top poster artist of that era. John was a founder member of the Thirty Club.

Harwood, Leslie

Born in Lancashire, Leslie was another Old Alleynian who had found his way into the advertising business. For many years he worked closely with Percy Burton as a Director of P. C. Burton & Co., St. James's Advertising & Publishing Co., and the London Press Exchange when that merger was effected.

During the first World War, we worked together for a short time at the War Office.

Higham, Sir Charles

Charlie Higham was one of the outstanding personalities of his era. Born within the sound of Bow Bells, he emigrated to the States, where, he used to boast, he held as many jobs as Heinz had varieties. Returning to England somewhere about 1906 or 1907, he joined Herbert Morgan at W. H. Smith's, but in a little while he broke away and formed

C. F. Higham Ltd., where he had the distinction of giving Ethel Mannin her first taste for literature.

For his work under Sir Eric Geddes in the first World War he subsequently received the K.B.E. He was a real orator, as distinct from just a good speaker.

He could be impetuous and was actually rash enough to offer me a job in early 1914. Whether I was wise or foolish in refusing it is anybody's guess.

Charlie died, poor chap, an unhappy death from cancer before doctors knew how to relieve the pain.

Imber, Horace

Tall, well dressed, sometimes apt to wear a stock, Horace's stature alone would have marked him out in a crowd, but with it he combined personality and ability. Advertisement Manager of the *Evening News* and later Advertisement Director of Associated Newspapers he was always referred to by Northcliffe as 'Lord Imber'. Despite which it was, I believe, in his reign that Northcliffe in his declining years suddenly announced that the Head Porter was to be censor of all advertising in the Carmelite House newspapers.

Leaving Carmelite House he became Advertisement Manager of the *Daily Chronicle*. He was, of course, a prominent member of the 1923 delegation to Atlantic City.

Johnson, Alfred

Of how or when Alfred Johnson invaded the advertising business, I have no knowledge. By the time I really got to know him he was well entrenched as Advertisement Manager of George Newnes Ltd., before they amalgamated with Pearsons some time before the first World War. He had his foibles but despite them he was very likeable. One of his foibles only became noticeable when he took you out to lunch or dinner. He would order a beautiful meal but when it was served he would proceed to send every dish back to the chef as not being cooked properly.

It was an education in *La Cuisine*, but it did not make for a pleasurable meal.

Kettle, George W.

In 1905 George Kettle was Advertising Manager of Maple's, the furnishers, and also of the Frederick Hotels, which Maple's owned. In that capacity he met Senator Edge, head of the Dorland Agency in the States. Edge who had for some time wanted to open a London office, took a fancy to Kettle and asked him to become its head, offering him £600 a year in place of the £400 he was getting at Maple's.

That was the start of Dorland Advertising Ltd. in two rooms at 151 Strand. Their main business was to act as representatives of American publications but they started with at least one real account, the Frederick Hotels, who still remain a client.

After the first World War Kettle, assisted by Julian Marks, worked out the demobilisation plans.

Kettle was quite a character. One day feeling he needed a Coat of Arms, he had his studio design a beautiful plate glass window with the motto *Qui Tel*, which still exists at Dorland House.

His hobby was weight lifting at which he won the Sandow Gold Medal.

George never really got over the tragic death of his younger daughter. He had a lovely house near the River with a beautiful lily pond. Throwing a seventeenth birthday party for her, he had the pond surrounded by fairy lights. His daughter jumped on to the parapet, overbalanced, grabbed at the cable and was instantly electrocuted.

Lawrence, T. B.

An employee of Carter Paterson, until Nationalisation the firm whose 'C.P.' sign in a housewife's window would ensure a call from the van driver or his mate to collect the parcel, 'T.B.' was the first to appreciate the advertising value of these mobile poster sites. Somehow or other, he secured a twenty-year contract from Carter Paterson, started his own business and made a lot of money. T.B. was the founder and for a long time conductor of the Fleet Street Choir.

He was also notable for his invariable habit of wearing brown boots with button tops.

The Advertising Agency he subsequently formed was nothing like as successful as his choir.

Leigh, Rowland

'Rowley' comes into this chapter as one of the 'characters' of the Street. He was for years a successful outside man on the *Daily Telegraph*. Every morning he would drive up to the office from Streatham or somewhere in a horse and trap. He would go his rounds in it and return to the office with the fruits of his labours.

Then home.

'Rowley' was, of course, only one of many who used that form of transport, but his horse was said to know its way to the office and home without any guidance from its master.

This was unique and, not infrequently, a godsend.

Millikin, Stephen

Stephen Millikin's first business job was in the wine vaults of Spiers and Pond. Some urge made him write some advertisements for them, which were received with sufficient favour to make him seek a job with Smith's Advertising Agency. After a period there he came into prominence as Advertising Manager of *The Times* edition of the *Encyclopaedia Britannica*.

Thence he went to Associated Newspapers as head of the new Ideas and Development Department they were setting up to assist the space selling department by supplying suggestions which would help its representatives to persuade advertisers to book space. (Agents did not particularly like this but it worked.)

After some years of running this department he became

Advertisement Manager of the *Daily Mail* and finally Advertisement Director of Associated Newspapers.

Morgan, Sir Herbert

In 1904, H. E. Morgan was working for Spottiswoode & Co., the printers. When John Spottiswoode broke away to start the Spottiswoode Advertising Agency, 'H.E.' went to W. H. Smith & Sons to do a similar job and did it very well. A tiny but still extant relic of his existence is the oval 'W.H.S.' symbol the firm uses to this day.

Someone else can fill in the gaps to the first World War. 'H.E.' came into prominence in the early days of that war as the promoter of the slogan: 'Business as Usual', which had quite a vogue till it fell terribly out of favour as being, firstly, terribly untrue and, secondly hopelessly inappropriate.

Despite this 'gaffe' Morgan was offered an important P.R.O. type of job in one of the Ministries and for his work there he was the second advertising man to receive a Knighthood.

Sometime after the war, following a brief period at the *Telegraph*, he became one of Levers' Managing Directors, being mainly in charge of MacFisheries, a concern which had a somewhat stormy passage, until it turned into the money-maker that it is today.

But 'H.E.s' most profitable achievement was to be Chairman of the Company when Smith's Potato Crisps first became a public company.

Murray, George

George Murray joined Pool's Advertising Service in 1894, and was its chief long before its name was changed to George Murray (Advertising) Ltd. This change according to George had nothing to do with his personal vanity. It was, he told me, because the old name was taken by some possible clients as indicating that it specialised in Football Pools and by others as being a subsidiary of Littlewood's or Vernon's.

George was very able and a very hard worker. Half an

hour before he was due to leave the office for his train to Southend, he would have a boy standing by, telling off the minutes as the clock ticked on.

Nind, E. T.

Teddy Nind became Advertisement Manager of Pearson's about the same time as Alfred Johnson was his opposite number at Newnes. For years they were desperate competitors, though very great personal friends.

In this connection Le Bas, when he was appointed director of the combined firms, told me that he had formed a much higher opinion of Nind's ability than he had ever had before.

Nind was for a long time Honorary Secretary of the Aldwych.

Osborne, Edward

Teddy Osborne was the first to demonstrate that the City of Manchester could really be a force in national advertising. The agency he started, Osborne Peacock, meant quite a lot to the newspapers. A very cheery bloke, Teddy had one habit which could be embarrassing. He would carry a lot of money about with him. Once at an Aldwych meeting at Sandy Lodge, he discovered at the tenth hole that he had left £100 in the Locker Room. I have never played eight holes so rapidly or so unsuccessfully. But Teddy made up for it at the nineteenth.

Pharaoh, Herbert Cornelius

Pharaoh's first advertisement managership was on the *Amateur Photographer* which he left to take over the *Sunday Referee*. Subsequently he became Advertisement Manager of the ill-fated *Tribune*. Old timers will remember Pharaoh among other things by his immaculate and carefully kept 'Imperial'.

Revely, Vernon J.

Destined originally for the Church, 'V.J.' somehow or other found himself working for Oetzman's, the Hampstead

Road furniture firm, then one of the most consistent advertisers. From there he went to the Charing Cross Bank, who were using a firm called W. L. Erwood Ltd. as advertising agents.

When W. L. Erwood Ltd. found itself in financial difficulties in 1896 or 1897, Reveley moved in and took the agency over. According to the *Advertising World*, he had a staff of one —W. J. Fitzgerald.

On the same authority Reveley was the man responsible in June 1904 for getting the agents together with the result that the first Incorporated Society of Advertising Agents was formed early the next year.

'V.J.' was Chairman of the Aldwych for several years. It was there I got to know him which led in 1923 to W. L. Erwood Ltd., becoming Erwoods Ltd., and my joining the reconstructed company where I found myself in daily and always congenial collaboration with the same Fitzgerald. 'Fitz' as he was known throughout the Street retired a year ago to my great regret and that of all his other friends.

Richardson, Arthur

After starting as a schoolmaster, Arthur Richardson joined the firm of Edward Lloyd Ltd., publishers of *Lloyds Weekly News* in 1898. It had the largest circulation of any Sunday newspaper, indeed of any newspaper in the country. In 1895 it was credited with a sale of 930,000 as compared with the 150,000 of the *News of the World.*

When the paper was sold to the *Daily Chronicle* group he continued as its Advertisement Manager and of the *Chronicle* and London Advertisement Manager of the *Edinburgh Evening News.*

Even in those days of frock coats and silk hats, Richardson prided himself as being the best-dressed man in Fleet Street, and, whatever the season, he could always be depended upon to be wearing a buttonhole.

Riddell, Baron of Walton

Not everybody really liked Lord Riddell, but it is difficult for a man to be so outstandingly successful without, at times, seeming ruthless. And it certainly was a record of success to rise from a little country lawyer in Wales to be the owner and guiding spirit of the newspaper with the largest nett sale in the World. In 1895 the circulation claimed by the *News of the World* was 150,000 and its advertising rate was a not very rigid nine shillings an inch. Its latest A.B.C. figure is over 7,000,000.

This alone would be a claim to fame. To attain his importance in political circles and to crown it with a peerage was another.

Riddell had an amazing memory for faces. As a lad I was thrilled to the core when, a year after giving me a ten-minute interview for *Printers' Ink*, he recognised me at a Sphinx Club Dinner and said how pleased he was to know that I was joining the Caxton of which he was a director.

Riddell and Le Bas of that Company were bosom friends for years, but their personalities were too dominating to let them live in 'each other's pockets' for ever.

And one day they fell out. When they did, they did it properly. Their friends were horrified to hear of impending actions and cross-actions and spent months trying to get the quarrel healed, but they never succeeded. They did however secure a sort of armistice agreement whereby each withdrew his actions and resigned from the other's companies. The one thing Le Bas would not resign from was Walton Heath Golf Club. It was, as a matter of fact, only by the skin of my teeth that I escaped being right in the middle of the row.

Robertson, W. B.

I believe 'W.B.' was a Canadian-Scot. I first heard of him and first met him when I was Advertising Manager of the Caxton Publishing Co., and he was boss of the Educational Book Co., a rival concern established by the Amalgamated Press. He was one of the many able advertising men turned out by Walter Martin's stable at what became the Carlyle Club. Walter Martin had realised the possibilities of selling cigars and cigarettes by mail from the Channel Isles, where the duty was, if not NIL, at least much smaller than if sold from anywhere in England. He built up a very big business which was eventually taken over by Rothman's.

Walter Martin himself was rather too fond of the gambling facilities provided by the romantic little State of Monaco. Meanwhile before he died, he had trained quite a few very able advertising men. 'W.B.' was one of them and it was a loss to Advertising when he went home to his empty house at Hampstead and was the victim of a German bomb.

Robinson, A. Wardle

Writing this in 1958 it is a tragic coincidence that the two famous Advertising Managers of Lyons should pass over within a week of each other. Wardle Robinson was the first to achieve fame in that capacity. Starting as a technical journalist, he joined Lyons shortly before the first World War with the job of 'publicising' the Strand Corner House. Then came a period in France as an officer in the Gunners. Rejoining Lyons in 1919 he produced some quite outstanding advertisements, particularly a series for the Trocadero. Reproduced today, they could even secure Layton awards.

Wardle left Lyons in 1925 to join Beaverbrook's papers and helped to increase the sales of the *Daily Express* to a million.

On this job he had the distinction of bringing Tetrazinni to England to give her first broadcast.

For a short period he was controlling editor of the *Advertising World*.

Russell, Thomas

There has never been anybody in the advertising business to whom I owe so much as I do to Thomas Russell, not because of what he did for me so much as because of what he taught me. My first knowledge of him was when he was Advertising Manager of John Morgan Richards Ltd., in its day the biggest distributor of American—and other—'Patent' medicines in this country. Russell left them to become Advertisement Manager of *The Times.* When he resigned that arduous post, he set up as the first Advertisement Consultant in Britain, and in that capacity he remained the leader of the profession until his death. His son, McDonough Russell, still waves the family standard and I cannot help treasuring a recent letter from him quoting his mother as saying, 'Ah yes! The Boy Field, as your father always called him, I have never met anybody in my life with whom I enjoyed dancing quite so much as with Eric Field.' Tempora Mutantur! She should try it now.

Salt, J. H.

Jack Salt is one of the many who are pleasant, but, alas, vague memories to me. I knew him as a tall, charming personality and Advertisement Manager of *T.P.'s Weekly.* He played an important part in the starting and conduct of 'N.A.B.S.'

Simonis, Henry

For several years Advertisement Manager of the *Morning Leader*, a daily with definitely Liberal tendencies. When it was merged with the *Daily News*, he went with it. Despite the limp from which he suffered for years, he was always cheery and encouraging to his younger colleagues, including his own younger brother, the Freddie Simonis who became Advertisement Manager of the *Daily Express* and the *Sunday Express* in the latter's earlier days.

Somerville, Roy V.

Roy Somerville's great and lasting tribute is the *Punch* that we know today. Before he left the *Delineator* to become Advertisement Manager of *Punch* in 1911, the paper found it difficult to sell its space at £25 a page and the management believed that if it carried more than eight pages it would lose most of its readership. Under Somerville's able direction, with the invaluable help of Marion Jean Lyon—because Somerville was almost crippled—the paper took a new lease of life and has never looked back. It is a classic example of the fact that advertisements of the right type can play a big part in creating sales of the paper itself.

Strong, James

'Jimmy Strong' was one of the stalwarts of the Advertising Agencies right up to and after the first World War. A director of C. Mitchell & Co., he was for its first nine years Chairman of the first Association of British Advertising Agents and an original subscriber to the I.P.A. He was also an ardent supporter of N.A.B.S. For several years before his death he was a sick man but he never allowed it to be apparent in his treatment of others.

Swann, L. Hartland

Originally a schoolmaster, Hartland Swann first became known in advertising circles as Advertising Manager of Icilma. This beauty product, used at that time to be advertised with a very strong suggestion that its beautifying properties derived from the waters of a mysterious Tunisian spring. Eventually it was bought by Lever's and Swann became one of the Managing Directors of the great organisation. He was an able and at times witty speaker and played a prominent part in organised Advertising, holding among other posts that of first President of the short-lived British Association of Advertising.

Teasdale, W. M.

Teasdale came into Advertising from an unusual stable. Who it was who discovered in a railway clerk at York the ability to handle the job of Advertisement Director of a large group of provincial newspapers and a couple of Nationals, I do not know. But somebody did and Teasdale justified his judgment. He soon became a figure in Advertising circles. As a speaker he was a shade dour but he was respected by all who knew him.

Warren, W. B.

One of the founders and for several years Chairman of the Advertisers Protection Society (progenitor of I.S.B.A.), Warren was a well-known character in the pre-war period. In those days his firm, Burge, Warren & Ridgley, was quite a prominent advertiser of fountain pens. A founder and very popular member of the Aldwych he was a back-marker in the Club's billiards matches as his opponents learned to their cost, including me.

Wetton, George

For years Advertisement Manager of the *Daily Express*, George was among other things a clever amateur conjurer. He was also an able controller of the then not very successful competitor of the *Daily Mail*. Jealous of the reputation of the whole front pages of the latter and failing to persuade his proprietor to change the front page of the *Express* from news to advertisements, he succeeded in being given the back page and of having the paper distributed folded 'back to front'. This unusual arrangement first came into effect in December 1910. It lasted, I think, up to the first World War.

Williams, A. H.

'Billy Williams', as everybody called him, first crossed my path as Advertising Manager of Selfridge's and a member of the Thirty Club. Selfridge's opening whole page advertisements were quite outstanding in their day. Some of them can still be seen framed on the staircases of the Store and for typography and artwork, as will be obvious from some of the illustrations to this book, they would pass muster today. One thing Bill did for the Club was to have its members invited to the fabulous parties Selfridge's used to throw on Election nights. To me it was great fun to travel to the States in 1924 with Bill and his charming wife, Bess. After leaving Selfridge's he started the 'Aims of Industry' which still flourishes.

Appendix 1
A few Early Advertisements

Originally I had not envisaged this story having any illustrations because the difficulties in the way of providing a representative selection of early advertisements would have made it an almost impossible task.

My publishers thought it would be incomplete without at least a few specimens.

The problem then arose as to where to secure worthwhile examples of advertisements in the period I have endeavoured to cover.

Ultimately we decided that as the *Daily Mail* had pioneered most of the early developments I should seek their help.

With their readily granted collaboration, this book closes with a few specimens of the kind of advertising employed in what was, in the early 1900's, our most important medium as well as of some of the popular typefaces of the period.

The first whole front page . . . Coronation Day, 11 August 1902

The last whole front page of a single advertiser,
1 September 1939

Daily Mail.

Daily Circulation Five Times as Large as That of Any Penny London Morning Journal.

A PAGE FOR LADIES. SEE BELOW.

NO. 2,635. MONDAY, SEPTEMBER 26, 1904. ONE HALFPENNY.

SPECIAL THIS WEEK.

Thos. Wallis & Co.

BEST HOUSE IN LONDON FOR ALL KINDS OF

Household Drapery & Linens.

SHEETINGS, Linen:

SHEETINGS, Cotton, Plain:

SHEETINGS, Cotton, Twilled:

CALICO and LONGCLOTHS:

FLANNEL, Real Welsh, all Wool:

FLANNEL, Saxony, Fine Make:

FLANNEL, Shirtings, all Wool:

FLANNEL, Shirtings, Union:

FLANNEL, Molleton, for Dressing Gowns:

FLANNEL, Molleton, Single Width:

FLANNELETTES, in any Plain Colours:

FLANNELETTES, in Stripes and Floral Designs.

FLANNELETTES, Safety Non-Flam.:

HUCKABACK, all Linen:

CRASH TOWELLING:

CARRIAGE PAID ON ALL ORDERS VALUE 20s.

THOS. WALLIS & Co., Ltd., HOLBORN CIRCUS, LONDON, E.C.

Important Notice FOR THIS WEEK.

PLUMMER RODDIS LTD.

HAVE PLEASURE IN ANNOUNCING THAT THEY ARE NOW MAKING A SPECIAL DISPLAY

WEINGARTEN'S

Of Weingarten's World Famous "Erect Form" and "La Vida" Corsets. They are a revelation to the modern woman. They come in over forty distinct models. There's a particular model for your individual figure.

"ERECT FORM."

"LA VIDA."

PLUMMER RODDIS Ltd., LONDON, W.

Special Attraction.

"PIRLE" COSTUMES

Do not SPOT or COCKLE with RAIN.

From the LEADING DRAPERS.

Shopping By Post.

We remind our readers that all goods advertised on this page may be purchased through the post. Remittance covering the cost should be enclosed with the order in each case. Customers may rely on their instructions being carefully carried out, and the advertisement manager is assured that all goods are accurately described and will be despatched promptly on receipt of order.

PETER JONES, Ltd.

NEW MATERIALS AUTUMN DRESSES.

AUTUMN DRESS MATERIALS

PETER JONES, Ltd.

Lotus Boots

Write for booklet

THE LONDON GLOVE COMPANY,

GLOVES & HOSIERY

SPECIAL AUTUMN SHOW

Ladies' Costumes

IN TWO DAYS.

PRESCOTT'S DUBLIN.

J. ROSENBAUM & SONS,

MAPLE & CO

TOTTENHAM COURT ROAD LONDON AND PARIS

THE LARGEST FURNISHING ESTABLISHMENT IN THE WORLD

BEDROOM FURNITURE

900 SUITES TO CHOOSE FROM 900

25,000 BEDSTEADS 25,000

SANITARY BEDDING

DINING ROOM FURNITURE

In Good Taste, yet Not Costly

MODEL RESIDENTIAL FLATS

One of the Most Interesting Sights in Town

MAPLE & CO

THE LARGEST FURNISHING ESTABLISHMENT IN THE WORLD

WM. WHITELEY, LTD.,

Important Announcement.

SPECIAL 3 DAYS' SALE

OF

Autumn Model Costumes, Coats and Skirts, Mantles, Jackets, and Fur Coats and Capes, also Children's Costumes & Mantles,

AT ABOUT

Half the Usual Prices.

ON

Tuesday, Wednesday, and Thursday, SEPTEMBER 27th, 28th, and 29th.

The stocks value over £8,000 and in most cases are original Paris, Vienne and Berlin Models. Owing to their great variety it is impossible to adequately describe them, but an idea of their value may be gained from the fact that they were originally marked at from 3 to 26 Guineas and will now be sold at from 1½ to 15 Guineas.

WM. WHITELEY, LTD.,

WESTBOURNE GROVE AND QUEEN'S ROAD, LONDON, W.

DEBENHAM and FREEBODY.

FEATHER STOLES

The Largest Stock in London. New Shapes, New Shades, and New Makes for Autumn and Winter Wear; extra heavy and thick. The comfort, warmth and effect of a fur wrap at less than one quarter the price.

Rich Feather Stoles, Price, 10/6, 16/6, 24/6, 27/6, 29/6, 42/-, 55/6, 63/-.

White Feather Stoles, Prices, 25/6, 34/6, 42/- to 63/-.

"Moleskin" Shade Feather Stoles, Prices, 29/6, 36/6, 42/-, 49/6.

Clipped Ostrich Stoles, Prices, 13/11, 19/6, 25/6, 42/-.

Real Ostrich Stoles, Prices, 16/6, 19/6, 29/6, 36/6, 49/6 to 7 Gns.

Coque Feather Boas, in White or Grey. Price, 12/6.

FEATHER STOLE, Price, 16/6. RICH COQUE BOA, Price, 12/6.

REAL OSTRICH STOLE, Price, 16/6. Extra Length, price 25/6. CLIPPED OSTRICH STOLE, Price, 13/11. Extra long and full 19/6.

DEBENHAM and FREEBODY, WIGMORE STREET, LONDON, W.

The first whole front page of Drapers, 26 September 1904

W. IZZARD'S GARDENING FEATURE IN PAGE 15

Daily Mail

FOR KING AND EMPIRE

Britain's Last Warning

SATURDAY, SEPTEMBER 2, 1939. ONE PENNY

OETZMANN

Examples of A.R.P. REQUIREMENTS

Order at Once—Stocks are Limited

CHENILLE CURTAINS

SCOTCH CHENILLE CURTAINS

OETZMANN & Co. Ltd.

PETTITS SPECIAL BARGAINS

For late Holidays and early Autumn

Charming Full Figure FROCK 14/6

TWO-PIECE 10/-

Full Figure TWO-PIECE 10/6

FROCK 7/6

PONTINGS

POSTAL SERVICE

If circumstances make it impossible to come to Pontings, remember that you can always keep in touch with Britain's best values through the post.

Whatever the circumstances, we shall endeavour to publish our Monthly Catalogue of Bargains as usual.

If your name is not already on our mailing list, or if you have moved, send your name and address TO-DAY.

A. R. P.

10,000 yards Black-Out material for curtains, blinds, doors, fanlights, etc. Use it also to protect your furniture—It's waterproof.

Black rubberising on a cotton foundation. Note the width: 70 ins. wide. 2/- Per yard.

PONTINGS, The House for Value, KENSINGTON, LONDON, W.8.

GREAT KNITTING FORTNIGHT AT PARNELLS

PATONS & BALDWINS

SCOTCH FINGERING · DOUBLE CREPE · SPECIAL RUG WOOL

5/4 · 5/10 · 2/9

ALL-WOOL VELOUR DRESSING GOWN 13/11

PARNELLS LTD., WILTON ROAD, VICTORIA, S.W.1

It's really time you tried a pair—

GRENFELL ★ GARMENTS BY GLANSON

GRENFELL GOLF JACKETS RAINCOATS AND SPORTSWEAR

You're as old as your feet!

RESTCOTS

NURSERY FURNITURE

MATERNITY WEAR

HITCHINGS

THE SUPERLATIVE BABY COACH

BOTH give you BENSON ACCURACY!—

EITHER can be yours for only 3/- with order

BENSON'S CATALOGUES FREE!

FLEET ELECTRICS of Regent St.

England's Largest Rebuilt Cleaner Firm!

G.E.C. MAGNET 59/6

GOBLIN 59/6

ELECTROLUX 59/6

10/- for YOU! 10/- for YOU! 10/- for YOU!

SEND COUPON & SAVE 10/-

HOOVER 80/-

59/6

THE PERFECT ULSTER

WOVEN CHECK BACK

West of England

Arch Moulded Shoes

CHURCH & CO. LTD. NORTHAMPTON

The last whole front page of all,
2 September 1939

DAILY MAIL, MONDAY, OCTOBER 27, 1902.

PURVEYORS OF BOVRIL
By Royal Warrant to
HIS MAJESTY THE KING.

Used by the Highest in the Land.

Bovril Helped Holbein on his Famous Channel Swim.

Given to Rescued Miners at the Forest of Dean Colliery.

Gillespie Takes a 90 Mile Walk on Bovril.

Bovril in South Africa.

Another Bovril War Picture.

Continually Making History.

PURVEYORS
TO
H.M. LEOPOLD II.,
KING OF THE BELGIANS.

The first whole page of Bovril,
27 October 1902

Daily Mail

Daily Circulation Five Times as Large as That of Any Penny London Morning Journal

Mr. PUNCH

Page 8.

LONDON. MANCHESTER. PARIS. ONE HALFPENNY.

Selfridge's by Night

BY Night as well as Day Selfridge's will be a centre of attraction. Contrary to the usual custom after closing time, the windows will not be obscured by blinds, but brilliantly lit up every Evening until Midnight.

These twenty-one windows, twelve of which are fronted with the largest sheets of plate glass in the world, will be frequently redressed, and will present a constant pageant of prevailing Fashion. We hope by beautiful setting and study of harmonious colouring to give pleasure to the artistic sense of every passer by, and to make the "Window Shows at Selfridge's in Oxford Street" worth a considerable detour to see.

Three specimens of the inaugural advertisements announcing the opening of Selfridge's in March 1909. Selfridge's took 6 whole pages and 3 quarter-pages in 9 publishing days

Daily Mail

Daily Circulation Five Times as Large as That of Any Penny London Morning Journal.

"Fashions For All."

RED MAGAZINE

LONDON. MANCHESTER. PARIS. ONE HALFPENNY.

Courtesy.

OF SERVICE COURTEOUS

THE "SELFRIDGE SERVICE," as we aim to make it, is not to be mere superficial courtesy. That kind has, of course, its many uses, and smooths the "give and take" of daily life, but the "Selfridge Service," emanating from a clearer thought of its commercial necessity, purposes to go deeper.

It aims to establish a cordial "entente" between Buyer and Seller, and so must be attentive, equable, suave and sincere. It must perform a duty gladly. It must spare no pains or trouble to give satisfaction. It must be diplomatic, in making rough places smooth, in soothing irritation. It must right a wrong at once, and rectify mistakes gracefully. It must be dignified without being pompous, and perfectly respectful because self-respecting. Above all things it must be keenly intelligent and alert to simplify a Visitor's or a Customer's perplexities.

The "Selfridge Service" must be all these things, and more, to [illegible] in the term "well bred."

Real Courtesy in Service [illegible] to success, and we believe unalterably the old teaching: "It a man would be greatest of all, let him be the servant of all." This is as true to-day as ever, and as sound a principle in business as it is in morals.

SELFRIDGE & CO.
OXFORD STREET, LONDON, W.

THE FOLLOWING IS A LIST OF THE SELFRIDGE CARTOONS FOR TO-DAY'S LONDON PAPERS, MORNING AND EVENING:—

DIGNITY IN COMMERCE, by Garth Jones. SINCERITY, by John Millar. COURTESY, by E. J. Sullivan.

These three examples show no reluctance to utilise white space

Contrast this, and previous two examples, with opposite page

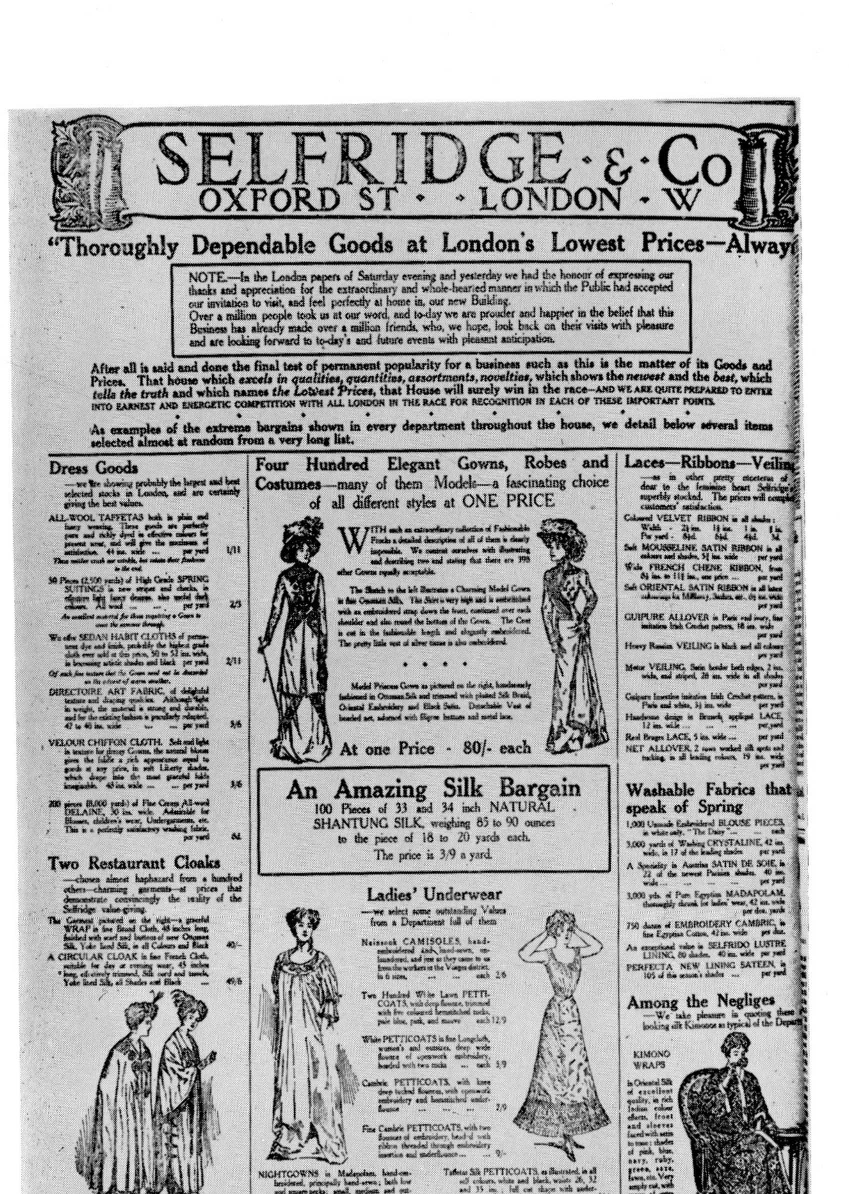

SELFRIDGE & Co
OXFORD ST · LONDON · W

"Thoroughly Dependable Goods at London's Lowest Prices—Always

NOTE.—In the London papers of Saturday evening and yesterday we had the honour of expressing our thanks and appreciation for the extraordinary and whole-hearted manner in which the Public had accepted our invitation to visit, and feel perfectly at home in, our new Building.
Over a million people took us at our word, and to-day we are prouder and happier in the belief that this Business has already made over a million friends, who, we hope, look back on their visits with pleasure and are looking forward to to-day's and future events with pleasant anticipation.

After all is said and done the final test of permanent popularity for a business such as this is the matter of its Goods and Prices. That house which *excels in qualities, quantities, assortments, novelties,* which shows the *newest* and the *best,* which *tells the truth* and which names *the Lowest Prices,* that House will surely win in the race—AND WE ARE QUITE PREPARED TO ENTER INTO EARNEST AND ENERGETIC COMPETITION WITH ALL LONDON IN THE RACE FOR RECOGNITION IN EACH OF THESE IMPORTANT POINTS.

As examples of the extreme bargains shown in every department throughout the house, we detail below several items selected almost at random from a very long list.

Dress Goods

—we are showing probably the largest and best selected stocks in London, and are certainly giving the best values.

ALL-WOOL TAFFETAS both in plain and fancy weaving. These goods are perfectly pure and richly dyed in effective colours for present wear, and will give the maximum of satisfaction. 44 ins. wide ... per yard 1/11

50 Pieces (2,500 yards) of High Grade SPRING SUITINGS in new stripes and checks, in effective light fancy designs, also useful dark colours. All wool ... ... per yard 2/3

We offer SEDAN HABIT CLOTHS of permanent dye and finish, probably the highest grade cloth ever sold at this price, 50 to 52 ins. wide, in becoming artistic shades and black per yard 2/11

DIRECTOIRE ART FABRIC, of delightful texture and draping qualities. Although light in weight, the material is strong and durable, and for the existing fashion is peculiarly adapted. 47 to 48 ins. wide ... per yard 3/6

VELOUR CHIFFON CLOTH. Soft and light in texture for dressy Gowns, the natural bloom gives the fabric a rich appearance equal to goods at any price, in soft Liberty shades, which drape into the most graceful folds imaginable. 48 ins. wide ... per yard 3/6

200 pieces (8,000 yards) of Fine Cream All-wool DELAINE, 30 ins. wide. Admirable for Blouses, children's wear, Undergarments, etc. This is a perfectly satisfactory washing fabric. per yard 8d.

Two Restaurant Cloaks

—chosen almost haphazard from a hundred others—charming garments—at prices that demonstrate convincingly the reality of the Selfridge value-giving.

The Garment pictured on the right—a graceful WRAP in fine Broad Cloth, 48 inches long, finished with scarf and buttons of new Ottoman Silk. Yoke lined Silk, all Colours and Black 40/-

A CIRCULAR CLOAK in fine French Cloth, suitable for day or evening wear, 45 inches long, ... trimmed, Silk cord and tassels, Yoke lined Silk, all Shades and Black ... 49/6

Four Hundred Elegant Gowns, Robes and Costumes—many of them Models—a fascinating choice of all different styles at ONE PRICE

WITH such an extraordinary collection of Fashionable Frocks a detailed description of all of them is clearly impossible. We content ourselves with illustrating and describing two and stating that there are 398 other Gowns equally acceptable.

The Sketch to the left illustrates a Charming Model Gown in fine Ottoman Silk. The Skirt is very high and is embellished with an embroidered strap down the front, continued over each shoulder and also round the bottom of the Gown. The Coat is cut in the fashionable length and elegantly embroidered. The pretty little vest of silver tissue is also embroidered.

• • • •

Model Princess Gown as pictured on the right, handsomely fashioned in Ottoman Silk and trimmed with plaited Silk Braid, Oriental Embroidery and Black Satin. Detachable Vest of beaded net, adorned with filigree buttons and metal lace.

At one Price - 80/- each

An Amazing Silk Bargain

100 Pieces of 33 and 34 inch NATURAL SHANTUNG SILK, weighing 85 to 90 ounces to the piece of 18 to 20 yards each.
The price is 3/9 a yard.

Ladies' Underwear

—we select some outstanding Values from a Department full of them

Nainsook CAMISOLES, hand-embroidered and hand-sewn, unlaundered, and just as they came to us from the workers in the Vosges district, in 6 sizes ... each 2/6

Two Hundred White Lawn PETTICOATS, with deep flounce, trimmed with five coloured hemstitched tucks, pale blue, pink, and mauve each 12/9

White PETTICOATS in fine Longcloth, women's and outsizes, deep wide flounce of openwork embroidery, headed with two tucks ... each 3/9

Cambric PETTICOATS, with knee deep tucked flounces, with openwork embroidery and hemstitched underflounce ... 7/9

Fine Cambric PETTICOATS, with two flounces of embroidery, headed with ribbon threaded through embroidery insertion and underflounce ... 9/-

NIGHTGOWNS in Madapolam, hand-embroidered, principally hand-sewn; both low and square necks; small, medium and outsizes ... each 4/6

Taffetas Silk PETTICOATS, as illustrated, in all self colours, white and black, waists 26, 32 and 35 ins.; full cut shape with underflounce, and stitched with silk ... 16/-

Telephone "Gerrard One"

All goods delivered Carriage Paid throughout the United Kingdom.

Laces—Ribbons—Veiling

—as in other pretty etceteras of dear to the feminine heart Selfridge's superbly stocked. The prices will compel customers' satisfaction.

Coloured VELVET RIBBON in all shades:

Width	2½ ins.	1½ ins.	1 in.	⅝ in.
Per yard	8½d.	6½d.	4½d.	3d.

Soft MOUSSELINE SATIN RIBBON in all colours and shades, 5½ ins. wide per yard

Wide FRENCH CHENE RIBBON, from 8½ ins. to 11½ ins., one price ... per yard

Soft ORIENTAL SATIN RIBBON in all latest colourings for Millinery, Sashes, etc., 6½ ins. wide per yard

GUIPURE ALLOVER in Paris and ivory, fine imitation Irish Crochet pattern, 18 ins. wide per yard

Heavy Russian VEILING in black and all colours per yard

Motor VEILING, Satin border both edges, 2 ins. wide, and striped, 28 ins. wide in all shades per yard

Guipure Insertion imitation Irish Crochet pattern, in Paris and white, 3½ ins. wide per yard

Handsome design in Brussels appliqué LACE, 12 ins. wide ... per yard

Real Bruges LACE, 5 ins. wide ... per yard

NET ALLOVER, 2 rows worked silk spots and tucking, in all leading colours, 19 ins. wide per yard

Washable Fabrics that speak of Spring

1,000 Unmade Embroidered BLOUSE PIECES, in white only, "The Daisy" ... each

3,000 yards of Washing CRYSTALINE, 42 ins. wide, in 17 of the leading shades per yard

A Speciality in Austrian SATIN DE SOIE, in 22 of the newest Parisian shades. 40 ins. wide ... per yard

3,000 yds. of Pure Egyptian MADAPOLAM, thoroughly shrunk for ladies' wear, 42 ins. wide per doz. yards

750 dozen of EMBROIDERY CAMBRIC, in fine Egyptian Cotton, 42 ins. wide per doz.

An exceptional value in SELFRIDO LUSTRE LINING, 80 shades. 40 ins. wide per yard

PERFECTA NEW LINING SATEEN, in 105 of the season's shades ... per yard

Among the Negliges

—We take pleasure in quoting these looking silk Kimonos as typical of the Depart

KIMONO WRAPS

In Oriental Silk of excellent quality, in rich Indian colour effects, front and sleeves faced with satin to tone; shades of pink, blue, navy, ruby, green, saxe, fawn, etc. Very amply cut, with many of extra large size

16/8

Selfridge's first *selling* advertisement, 22 March 1909

THE only English morning Journal certifying the exact number of copies actually sold daily.

Daily Mail

GREATER LONDON EDITION.

Daily Net SALE Six Times as Large as That of Any Penny London Morning Journal.

[illegible], JANUARY 15, 1914. LONDON. MANCHESTER. PARIS. No. [illegible] ONE HALFPENNY.

What the Army offers.

To all single men of good character between 18 and 25 years of age the Army offers good wages, good food, and unique opportunities for Sports and Games—the surest means of keeping a man fit for service in the field. Send the form below for a free copy of a 32-page illustrated book on "The Army and What it Offers."

HAVE you ever seriously thought about the advantages of the Army? Probably not, and most likely for the simple reason that you have never had placed before you the true facts of a soldier's life and the conditions of his service. If you will fill up and send in the form below you will receive a free copy of "The Army and What it Offers," a 32-page illustrated book that gives full details of life in the Army and tells of its many advantages and how to join it.

When you are considering your future you would do well to consider the Army and all the chances it offers you.

Soldiers' Wages.

What are you earning now, and what are your prospects in civil life? Can you look forward with certainty to getting more than 25s. a week if in a town, or 20s. if in the country? And even with these wages what have you left for yourself at the end of the week after paying for your lodging, for train or tram fares to your work, for your food, for your Insurance, and for the clothes and boots you wear while at work or at leisure?

And now consider the soldier. He is charged 3d. or 4d. a day for his groceries and vegetables, to meet which he is given a "Messing Allowance" of 3d. a day, and he has to pay 1½d. a week for his Insurance, but practically all the rest of his necessities are provided for him free—lodging, rations, and clothing. In the Infantry the average balance of pay at the disposal of a private soldier immediately after enlistment is 6s. 8½d. per week; after serving for 2 years, if in the First Class for Proficiency, a private has at his disposal 10s. 8½d., a Corporal 14s. 10½d., and a Sergeant 17s. 9d.

Soldiers' Savings.

Remember, too, that if a soldier likes to save whilst he is with the Colours, he can do so to some purpose. An Infantry private drawing First Class Proficiency Pay could spend 4s. a week on himself, and if he put the balance of his pay in the Post Office Savings Bank could save in round figures £100 after 7 years' service. And there is another point—a man has opportunities whilst serving of learning work that will be useful to him when he leaves the Colours.

Promotion.

You have seen that a private is well off in the Army, but any steady and well-conducted soldier with ambition may well look forward to promotion and consequent increase of pay and improvement of position. The chance of being offered a Commission as Officer has now been made greater, and may certainly be considered as a possibility by any ambitious young man who joins the Army.

Soldiers' Holidays.

In civil life a man may be allowed a holiday of a week or a fortnight every year, and perhaps then only by losing his wages.

A soldier can usually depend on being given a holiday of at least a month each year, and in addition can often get leave of absence for a few days at other times. Whilst on leave and during the whole of his long holiday he receives his full daily rate of pay, and in addition gets 3s. 6d. a week to make up for the rations he receives free whilst in barracks.

Sports, Games, Etc.

In the Army a man has unique opportunities for all kinds of sports and games, such as he can get in no other profession to anything like the same extent. Every encouragement is given to the soldier to play cricket, football, and hockey, grounds being provided for these sports in all garrisons. In most garrisons there is a well-equipped gymnasium, and the soldier's physical training and development are everywhere carefully supervised by expert Instructors. Shooting and swordsmanship form part of the soldier's actual work, and athletic sports with good prizes are often held.

Weekly Pay

of Privates in the Regular Army,

in addition to Lodging, Rations and Clothing.

[illegible]

	On Enlistment	After 2 years including proficiency pay
Household Cavalry	14/-	15/9 to 17/6
Cavalry	9/11	11/8 to 13/5
Royal Horse Artillery		
Gunner	11/1	12/10 to 14/7
Driver	10/6	12/3 to 14/-
Royal Field Artillery	10/2½	11/11½ to 13/8½
Royal Garrison Artillery	10/2½	11/11½ to 13/8½
Foot Guards	9/4	11/1 to 12/10
Infantry of the Line	8/9	10/6 to 12/3

The Pay of Soldiers in the Royal Engineers, Army Service Corps, Royal Flying Corps, Royal Army Medical Corps, Army Ordnance Corps, and all other branches will be found in the free illustrated booklet.

Seeing the World.

The soldier has exceptional opportunities of seeing the world free of cost to himself. The British Army is in garrison all over the Empire, and Gibraltar, Malta, Egypt, Hong Kong, Channel Islands, India, the West Indies, and South Africa may all be visited by him.

Comfortable Quarters.

In all regimental barracks there is a recreation-room with billiard and bagatelle tables, newspapers, and indoor games; there is a well-stocked library, a canteen fitted with coffee bars, and in the evening there is often a concert or other entertainment in barracks, given by local or outside talent. In the Army, too, the meals are better and more varied than those of the ordinary civilian; the food provided is of excellent quality, it is well cooked, and there is always enough.

For the Skilled Workman or Clerk.

If you have a knowledge of some trade, it will probably help you to earn more money in the Army. Certain Corps (Royal Engineers, Army Ordnance, Army Service, and Royal Flying Corps) are largely composed of men engaged in some trade, whilst in almost every regiment there are openings for carpenters, shoemakers, tailors, and shoeing-smiths, and a man who is a good clerk is practically certain of employment, with a very good chance of early promotion.

The Special Reserve.

A man who would like to receive a military training, so as to be able to serve his country in time of war, but who is not prepared to devote the whole of his time to soldiering, will probably find what he wants in the Special Reserve, a force which has taken the place of the old Militia, and in which retaining fees and bounties are paid on a good scale. The Special Reserve is open to men of 17 to 30, and some particulars of service in it are included in the book which will be sent on receipt of the Coupon printed below.

The remarks in the previous paragraphs, though they refer more particularly to the Regular Army, are equally applicable in many cases to service in the Special Reserve.

General Advantages.

Such, then, are some of the many advantages the Army offers to the ambitious man. Good pay, chances of promotion, long holidays, unique opportunities for games and sports, and travel to foreign parts—these are some of the benefits the Country gives a man in return for his services, while there is no career that can offer a man greater chances of distinction.

Write for the Free Book To-day.

If you are an ambitious man in want of a stirring life, send the Coupon below, with your name and address, for a free copy of "The Army and What it Offers"—a 32-page book, giving full details of life in the Army and the pay of the various regiments. It is well illustrated with photographs, and is a book that every man ought to read. Send the form below or a postcard to-day for a copy. It will be sent post free and without any obligation on your part. No stamp is needed for postage.

Or, if what you have read on this page has decided you to enlist without further delay, write to, or call on, the nearest Recruiter, whose address you can obtain at any Post Office or Government Labour Exchange, and he will tell you what to do.

A FREE BOOK.

This coupon should be sent at once to avoid delay. Do not stamp the envelope, as no stamp is needed, but mark your envelope "O.H.M.S."

To the Secretary, War Office (Recruiting Dept.), Whitehall, S.W.

Please send me, free of charge and without any obligation on my part, a copy of the 32-page illustrated book, "The Army and What it Offers," giving particulars of the conditions of service in the Army.

NAME ....

(Send this form or a postcard mentioning this paper. No postage stamp needed.)

ADDRESS ....

....

"The Daily Mail."

The first real advertisement ever used by the Government, 15 January 1914

REGULAR READERS of "The Daily Mail" are insured for £250 against accidental death by drowning while BOATING or BATHING at any seaside resort in the United Kingdom, Channel Islands, or Isle of Man. For full details see inside.

Daily Mail

GREATER LONDON EDITION.

Daily Net SALE Six Times as Large as That of Any Penny London Morning Journal.

THURSDAY, APRIL 30, 1914. | LONDON. | MANCHESTER. | PARIS. | NO. 5,636. | ONE HALFPENNY.

Mr. Zog says "You don't often see a page as clean as this, do you? I've been using Zog."

Zog cleans paint.

A classic example of white space, 30 April 1914

[I believe Abdulla Cigarettes subsequently had one with even less type. The printers took a very poor view of this kind of advertisement]

THE DAILY MAIL, WEDNESDAY, AU

Your King and Country need you.

WILL you answer your Country's Call? Each day is fraught with the gravest possibilities, and at this very moment the Empire is on the brink of the greatest war in the history of the world.

In this crisis your Country calls on all her young unmarried men to rally round the Flag and enlist in the ranks of her Army.

If every patriotic young man answers her call, England and her Empire will emerge stronger and more united than ever.

If you are unmarried and between 18 and 30 years old will you answer your Country's Call? and go to the nearest Recruiter—whose address you can get at any Post Office, and

JOIN THE ARMY TO-DAY!

MONEY CRISIS.

change—much of it in bright new copper coin. This was, no doubt, in preparation for the extra demand for small change.

The first Government advertisement on the outbreak of the first World War, 5 August 1914

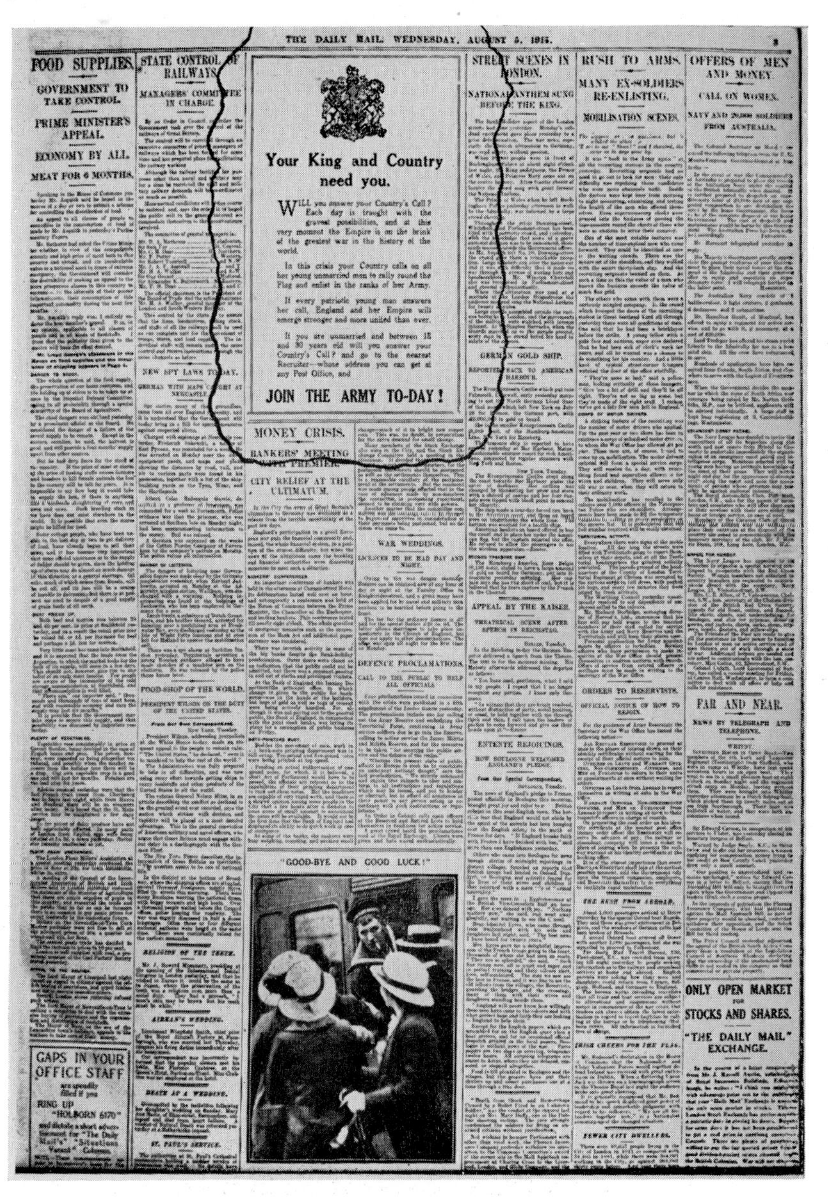

THE DAILY MAIL, WEDNESDAY, AUGUST 5, 1914.

FOOD SUPPLIES.

GOVERNMENT TO TAKE CONTROL.

PRIME MINISTER'S APPEAL.

ECONOMY BY ALL.

MEAT FOR 6 MONTHS.

STATE CONTROL OF RAILWAYS.

MANAGERS' COMMITTEE IN CHARGE.

NEW SPY LAWS TO-DAY.

FOOD-SHOP OF THE WORLD.

PRESIDENT WILSON ON THE DUTY OF THE UNITED STATES.

Your King and Country need you.

WILL you answer your Country's Call? Each day is fraught with the gravest possibilities, and at this very moment the Empire is on the brink of the greatest war in the history of the world.

In this crisis your Country calls on all her young unmarried men to rally round the Flag and enlist in the ranks of her Army.

If every patriotic young man answers her call, England and her Empire will emerge stronger and more united than ever.

If you are unmarried and between 18 and 30 years old will you answer your Country's Call? and go to the nearest Recruiter—whose address you can get at any Post Office, and

JOIN THE ARMY TO-DAY!

MONEY CRISIS.

BANKERS' MEETING WITH PREMIER.

CITY RELIEF AT THE ULTIMATUM.

WAR WEDDINGS.

LICENCES TO BE HAD DAY AND NIGHT.

DEFENCE PROCLAMATIONS.

CALL TO THE PUBLIC TO HELP ALL OFFICIALS.

"GOOD-BYE AND GOOD LUCK!"

STREET SCENES IN LONDON.

NATIONAL ANTHEM SUNG BEFORE THE KING.

GERMAN GOLD SHIP.

APPEAL BY THE KAISER.

ENTENTE REJOICINGS.

RUSH TO ARMS.

MANY EX-SOLDIERS RE-ENLISTING.

MOBILISATION SCENES.

ORDERS TO RESERVISTS.

OFFERS OF MEN AND MONEY.

CALL ON WOMEN.

FAR AND NEAR.

NEWS BY TELEGRAPH AND TELEPHONE.

ONLY OPEN MARKET FOR STOCKS AND SHARES.

"THE DAILY MAIL" EXCHANGE.

GAPS IN YOUR OFFICE STAFF are speedily filled if you RING UP "HOLBORN 6170" and dictate a short advertisement for "The Daily Mail's" "Situations Vacant" Columns.

The position the papers gave it

Your King and Country need you.

A CALL TO ARMS

AN addition of **100,000** men to His Majesty's Regular Army is immediately necessary in the present grave National Emergency.

Lord Kitchener is confident that this appeal will be at once responded to by all those who have the safety of our Empire at heart.

TERMS OF SERVICE.

General Service for a period of 3 years or until the war is concluded. Age of enlistment between 19 and 30.

HOW TO JOIN.

Full information can be obtained at any Post Office in the Kingdom or at any Military Depot.

God Save the King.

How Kitchener re-wrote it, 11 August 1914

Appendix 2

Display types of the period

Figure 1

The Beginning of Display Advertising. The example of the *Daily Mail* catches on with *The Standard*. Reproduction, half-size, of first page from 'The Standard Advertisement Display Types' dated 15 May 1905. Somerville was subsequently the founder of the *Punch* advertising reputation.

Advertisement Offices, "The Standard" and "Evening Standard and St. James's Gazette" 23, St. Bride Street, London, E.C.

IN submitting to Advertisers and Advertising Agents this book of Display Advertising Types which have been put in stock for use in display advertisements in "The Standard" and "The Evening Standard and St. James's Gazette," particular attention is called to the following points:

That all the styles have been carefully selected with a view to harmonizing as completely as possible one with the other and without destroying that distinct individuality which every intelligent advertiser desires for his advertisements.

That the effort has been to supply advertisers with the fullest possible number of sizes of a comparatively few good advertising type faces, rather than to confuse them by a large assortment of styles of type with only a few sizes of each

That the well-balanced and attractive advertisement is built up most effectually by the use of ONE DISTINCT STYLE or face of type in its various sizes, with perhaps a catch or display line or two in some harmonious yet contrasting type, than by the use of many different styles of type. To illustrate turn to pages 3, 4, and 8B, and see how the Britannic and Britannic Italic series would harmonize and yet afford contrasts.

That by the use of this specimen book advertisers can plan their advertisements intelligently, specifying first the general style—as for instance, "Set in Britannic and Britannic Italic," leaving the proportions and sizes to the advertisement compositor, or if the advertiser desires to be more exact, and has the proper sense of type proportion, specifying the exact sizes each line is to be set in by number, as for instance, "set this line in No. —, this one in No. —"

That to set up a telling, attractive, distinctive advertisement is only possible when sufficient time to properly plan the work is allowed An advertisement can be easily set up in a rush at the last moment, but a *good* advertisement which will bring back to the advertiser proper return for his expenditure requires time to plan, time to set up, time to be submitted in proof—and alas, very frequently much more time to be—not corrected—but practically reset, because of lack of proper care in the preparation of copy.

That with good copy, promptly supplied, time to set it properly, intelligent selection of type, and prompt return of proofs, the Standard Advertisement Department can give in the mediums it offers the very highest value obtainable in the advertising field, especially if your goods are of a superior class.

That if advertisers who spend large sums for expensive space understood that the chief difficulty of the advertising manager of a leading newspaper is not to secure orders, but to secure copy and blocks for advertisements in time to permit submission even of a rough proof, and that this hurry to get in copy at the last moment in "any old shape" takes the bloom off much of the profit of their advertising, there would be some radical overhauling of the methods of their own advertisement departments and the copy departments of their advertising agents.

¶ Perhaps this book will make the work of preparing copy for "The Standard" and "The Evening Standard" easier, and help to get in the copy sooner. If it does even in the slightest degree, it will very much gratify

Yours truly,

ROY V. SOMERVILLE,

Advertisement Manager.

May 15th, 1905.

Figure 2

Typical display types of the period as shown in *The Standard* book of 1905. The Grots have since enjoyed a return to popularity in the middle fifties. The figures prefacing each type showing are the number of characters in the column measure, but no allowance is ever made for spaces, with some odd results.

GROTESQUE SERIES (continued)

Single Col.—Upper 23	Single Col.—Lower 29
THE STANDARD IS THE LEADING	The Standard is the leading daily 2

NO. 28—6 Pnt. Grotesque. Letters in line—Upper 70; lower 86

THE STANDARD IS THE LEADING DAILY MORNING NEWSPAPER IN THE WORLD. PRICE ONE PENNY. GOO

The Standard is the leading daily morning newspaper in the world. Price One Penny. Good leading articles

Single Col.—Upper 36	Single Col.—Lower 43
THE STANDARD IS THE LEADING DAILY MORNING N	The Standard is the leading daily morning newspape

ROMAN ANTIQUE SERIES.

NO. 29—30 Pnt. Rom. Ant. Letters in line—Upper 15; lower 23

THE STANDARD IS TH

The Standard is the leading

NO. 30—24 Pnt. Rom. Ant. Letters in line—Upper 18; lower 29

THE STANDARD IS THE LE

The Standard is the leading daily o

NO. 31—18 Pnt. Rom. Ant. Letters in line—Upper 23; lower 34

THE STANDARD IS THE LEADING

The Standard is the leading daily mornin

ATHENIAN SERIES.

NO. 32—42 Pnt. Athenian. Letters in line—Upper only 5

THE ST

Figure 3

The title page of S. H. Benson's *Facts for Advertisers*, an invaluable book of reference for those in the advertising and Press world of the Edwardian period. Many other books of reference have since appeared, but probably none command the affection of Benson's Facts, at half a guinea (net), from older members of the professions. Dated 1907-8 and reproduced actual size. Note the full point at end of all lines is *de rigueur*.

BENSON'S

FACTS

FOR

ADVERTISERS.

A collection of data on the subject of Press and Outdoor Publicity, useful to all interested or engaged in the profession or business of advertising.

(*With Maps.*)

HALF GUINEA (NET).

COMPILED AND PUBLISHED BY
S. H. BENSON, LTD., ADVERTISERS' AGENTS,
1, TUDOR STREET, LONDON, E.C.

1907-8.

Figure 4

Double-spread from the Benson *Facts for Advertisers* of 1907-8. The left-hand page gives cast-off of number of words in the single-column setting for each type size. Note first line of second paragraph which shows how rough and ready was the whole basis of calculation at this time. Some of the type names listed on the right-hand page have now passed into rightful oblivion.

Approximate Number of Words in 1 in. Single Column.—*contd.*

A single Column measuring 2¼ in. wide is taken.

Weak advertising brings very little profit, if any. How to put strength into an advertisement is an agent's daily problem. Advertising may be forceful in many ways ; loud thunder

Pica, 12 point, 29 words.

Weak advertising brings very little profit, if any. How to put strength into an adver

Great Primer, 18 point, 18 words.

Weak advertising brings very little profit, if any. How to put strength into an ad

Great Primer Condensed Sans., 18 point, 15 words.

Weak advertising brings very little profit, if any. How to put streng

Great Primer De Vinne, 18 point, 12 words.

96

SPECIMEN TYPE-FACES.

In the following pages a selection of type-faces will be found, suitable for newspaper and magazine advertisements. Many printers have their own type books, and from time to time new varieties of type are introduced. Up-to-date Printers can obtain any that may be required, but these here reproduced have been selected for their suitability for general use and will be found to meet all ordinary requirements.

To give a good example of the types chosen, they have been shown in all except the largest sizes, together with the figures of the same size and series. These latter are so chosen as to give approximately the number of the letters of the size they follow, which would fill (without spaces) one line of a 2¼-inch column. For ordinary calculations a space counts as a letter. But it should be remembered that letters vary greatly in width, so that lines would take many more or less letters according to the nature of the words used.

Below is a list of the type-faces which are shewn on the following pages :—

De Vinne Italic, Chantrey and Britannic will be found in 1906-1907 Edition.

Modern Roman.

Nonpareil (6 point).

MANCHESTER AND SAL 36 printing and purchase prin 48

Brevier (8 point).

NORTHUMBERLAN 27 prospectus rates prospe 40

Bourgeois (9 point)

NOTTINGHAMSH 25 magazines and revie 34

Long Primer (10 point)

HUDDERSFIELD 24 copy and designs co 32

Small Pica (11 point)

NEWCASTLE 22 ladies' papers 29

Pica (12 point)

EDINBURGH 19 newspaperdom 25

97

Figure 5

Another double-spread from Benson's *Facts* for 1907-8. This was the heyday of Cheltenham, the first type face to have a 'family' built round it, and thus establish an unchallenged supremacy in the cases of all printers for nearly a half-century. Reduced, as previous plate, about half-size. Note 'type names' in parenthesis after sizes. The point system inherited from the U.S.A. was just beginning to take root.

TYPE FACES.

Cheltenham Old Style.

6 point (Nonpareil).
MANCHESTER AND SA 32 printings and purchases printing 60

8 point (Brevier).
NORTHUMBERLAN 27 prospectus and rates prosp 47

10 point (Long Primer).
HUDDERSFIEL 22 copy and designs cop 40

12 point (Pica).
EDINBURGH 19 newspaperdom ne 35

14 point (English).
HALIFAX 15 advertisers adv 28

18 point (Great Primer).
OXFOR 13 posting post 24

24 point (2-Line Pica).
WIGA 10 papered 18

30 point (2-Line English).
YORI 8 ideasy 15

36 point (3-Line Pica).
AYS 6 magi 12

42 point (2-Line Double Pica).
SOI 5 ads 10

102

TYPE FACES.

Cheltenham Bold.

6 point (Nonpareil).
MANCHESTER AND SA 32 printing and purcnase 50

8 point (Brevier).
NORTHUMBERLAN 27 prospectus rates prosp 42

10 point (Long Primer).
HUDDERSFIEL 22 copy and design 32

12 point (Pica).
EDINBURGH 19 newspaperdom 28

14 point (English).
HALIFAX 15 advertisers 24

18 point (Great Primer).
OXFOR 12 bill-post 19

24 point (2-Line Pica).
WIGA10 paper 14

30 point (2-Line English).
YOR 8 idea 11

36 point (3-Line Pica).
AYR6 mag 9

48 point (4-Line Pica)
SO 5 ads 7

103

Figure 6

Interesting for two reasons: firstly, De Vinne, a great American printer at the turn of the century and type designer and writer, produced a range of types named after himself which had a long life, and indeed are still seen today in Press settings. Secondly, this reproduction half-size is from the *Type Specimens* of Spottiswoode & Co. Ltd. of 1913, the printing firm from which 'Spotts' the agency hived-off.

DE VINNE

60 POINT

MEDICINES
Retail Prices

54 POINT

PERFUMERY
Toilet Articles

48 POINT

ELEMENTARY
Highest Award

36 POINT

FAIRLY MODERATE
Investigation Officers

42

Figure 7

The *Daily Mail* in the early twenties produced another variant on the newspaper type specimen book. Entitled *The Daily Mail Instant-Index Type Book*, it provided a patented, centrally-indexed specimen book, with a long introduction about style with hints to intending advertisers—somewhat after the pattern of figure 1. Neither of the types shown is now much used, if at all, in the Press.

STANHOPE

142 8 PT. 25
THE BEST NEWSPAPER ADVERTISI
33
The Best Newspaper Advertising is that

143 10 PT. 18
THE BEST NEWSPAPER AD
27
The Best Newspaper Advertising

144 12 PT. 16
THE BEST NEWSPAPER
20
The Best Newspaper Adve

145 14 PT. 13
THE BEST NEWSPA
17
The Best Newspaper A

146 18 PT. 11
THE BEST NEWS
16
The Best Newspaper

147 24 PT. 8
THE BEST N
10
The Best New

148 30 PT. 7
THE BEST
9
The Best Ne

149 36 PT. 6
THE BES
7
Best New

151 48 PT. 4
THE B
5
The Be

CON. HARWARDEN OUTLINE

157 24 PT. 12
THE BEST NEWSP
16
The Best Newspaper

159 36 PT. 8
THE BEST N
11
The Best News

49

Figure 8

Another page from *The Daily Mail Type Book*, showing anticipation of the great revival in better-designed type faces. This was already well under way on the Continent, but was only beginning to be effective in England, and only after book-work had already begun to clean up. Cameo is still a good display for Press work and Clearface Bold continues to find its uses in both editorial and advertisement space.

CAMEO

906 18 PT. 9

THE BEST NE

12

The Best Newsp

907 24 PT. 8

THE BEST N

9

The Best Ne

908 30 PT. 6

THE BES

8

The Best N

909 36 PT. 5

THE BE

7

The Best

910 42 PT. 4

THE B

5

The Be

911 48 PT. 4

THEB

4

The B

CLEARFACE BOLD

926 18 PT. 11

THE BEST NEWS

15

The Best Newspape

927 24 PT. 9

THE BEST NE

11

The Best News

928 30 PT. 8

THE BEST N

10

The Best New

929 36 PT. 6

THE BES

8

The Best N

930 42 PT. 5

THE BE

7

The Best

931 48 PT. 4

THE B

6

The Bes

Index

Printed in Great Britain by
The Camelot Press Ltd., London and Southampton